Georgette

Peace by Piece

Phyllis Clemmons

Copyright © 2018

ISBN-13: 978-1727408423
ISBN-10: 172740842X
LCCN: 2018911091

Cover design image: by Phyllis Clemmons
Interior layout: by Phyllis Clemmons
Logo image: by Scott Baker
E-mail: phyllis.clemmons@hotmail.com
Cellular phone # 210 607-9112

DEDICATION

This book is dedicated to my dad, George Sawyer. I loved you then, I love you still. I always have, and I always will. Rest in peace.

FOREWORD

One indiscretion between two people was the catalyst that destroyed the lives of three families.

These families started out as good, law abiding citizens. They went to church, they were prominent figures in their careers and they were well respected in their communities.

However, the enemy planted a seed that would orchestrate a one night sexual encounter that would bring a harvest of deceit, lies, blackmail, revenge and ultimately, murder. This encounter would leave their lives in ruin.

ACKNOWLEDGEMENT

I would like to acknowledge a fellow author, Andrea Buckner, for her brave and courageous fight until the very end. She demonstrated the true meaning of friendship.

Once a week, she would pick up the phone and call me. Today, I can still hear her sweet voice as she spoke, "Hello lovely, I'm just calling to check on you."

Although it was a short friendship, as we only met last summer. Nevertheless, it left a strong and lasting impression on my life.

Thank you for allowing me to be a part of making one of your dreams come true. Rest in heaven, my friend.

Chapter 1

The Package

I was on my hands and knees inside of my bedroom closet looking for the mate to my favorite pumps, when I heard the doorbell ring. I stood up and bumped my head on the clothing bar. "Ouch!" I started walking toward the door, holding my head in hopes of relieving the pain. The doorbell rang again. I shouted, "O.k., I'm coming!" I snatched the door open. The mailman was standing there smiling, holding a box and his hand held signature gadget.

"Good morning, Diane Wakefield? I have a package for you. Sign here please." He held the machine out and I signed for the box. Thanking him, as we exchanged items. I gave him back the machine and he gave me the box. "Have a nice day," he turned and walked down the path. "You too," I said as I held the package with both hands, turned my back and kicked the door closed with my foot.

I sat the package down on the kitchen counter. I remember thinking to myself, *how strange, no return address is listed.* I reached in the drawer for the box cutter and glided it over the crease where the two flaps met in the middle. Opening the flaps, I was puzzled about the dry ice; *who would be sending me something packed in dry ice?*

I removed the dry ice and sat it on the kitchen counter. I lifted the bubble wrapped object from the box and tried to unravel it from its many layers.

I became frustrated with my slow progress and decided to get the scissors from the drawer to finish cutting it open. As the object became fully exposed, I dropped the contents like a hot potato and watched in horror as it rolled across the floor.

I couldn't believe what I was seeing. Was this some sort of sick Halloween trick? But it couldn't be as it was the middle of July.

I could hear someone screaming hysterically. It took a few seconds before I realized it was me. Tears streamed down my face. I was staring at the head from a body. It was the head of my sister, Georgette. Her eyes were wide open and a look of sheer terror was etched across her face.

Helpless, I sunk to the floor with my hands up to my face still screaming. I was sickened by the site but was unable to shift my gaze away from it. I could feel nausea rising up from my stomach. I tried to make it to the bathroom, but threw up just inside of the bathroom doorway.

I had not heard from my sister Georgette in three days. I called her cell a few times but it kept going straight to voicemail. I didn't think a lot of it at the time as it was not uncommon for Georgette to disappear for several days without communicating with anyone. She would eventually call a few days later wondering why I was, 'so bent out of shape.'

I could hear someone banging hard on the front door. I pulled myself up and ran past the kitchen in the direction of the banging. I was careful not to look in the direction of where the head had rolled to a stop. I didn't want to see my sister that way again.

I snatched the door open and there stood a police officer. He was concluding a conversation of some sort with the radio dispatcher. I fell into his arms still crying. He immediately stepped back and pulled me away from him, holding me at arms-length.

"Hey young lady, is everything alright here?" I was crying very hard as I attempted to tell him what happened, but he was not able to understand a word I said. "Whoa! Slow down, take a deep breath and try to tell me what's going on" He handed me a handkerchief and I began wiping my face and blowing my nose with it.

"Is anyone inside, I can talk to?" "No," I said. "I live alone." Okay, do you want to try telling me what happened here?" "She's in there." I pointed inside the house. "I mean her head is. I mean it was delivered by the postman in a box addressed to me."

The officer looked past me inside the house. Moving me aside, he unstrapped his gun holster and began cautiously entering through the front door while speaking into his radio again.

Everything seemed like a blur after that. More police officers, forensic people and a detective came. I sat on the sofa in the living room as they all huddled around Georgette's head. They were talking, taking pictures, writing notes, taping off the outside area.

A female officer handed me a glass of water. I took a few sips and set the glass on the coffee table. She sat down beside me and began asking questions about the box, about Georgette and if I knew of anyone who would want to hurt her. She wanted to know if my sister had any enemies, when was the last time I saw or heard from her. Questions, questions and more questions.

They finally left, taking Georgette's remains (such as they were) along with the box and told me to come down to police headquarters the following day, they had more questions.

A detective handed me his card and said he would be in touch. Finally, I was alone. I was shaking like a leaf. I was still holding the handkerchief, the officer had given me.

The tears began to roll down my face again. I knew I couldn't stay in that house tonight. I had to get out of there.

I suddenly remembered, I hadn't told my parents yet. I had to get to them before they heard about it from a stranger. They needed to hear the news about Georgette from me and not from some stranger. Besides, I had to get out of there.

I hurriedly tossed some things in an overnight bag. I decided to drive to my parents' to break the news. I had no idea what I would say. How do you tell your mother and father that their child is dead? I didn't know. I just knew, it was up to me to find a way.

I called my best friend Cynthia. She answered on the third ring. "Hey girl, what's up?" "Cynthia, something terrible has happened. Can I come over? I need a place to stay for a few days?" "Sure, what's going on?"

"I'll tell you when I get there. "Okay calm down, you sound hysterical. Do you want me to come get you?" "No, I'll be fine. I need to stop by my parents' house first. I should be at your place within the next hour or two. With concern in her voice Cynthia said, "Okay, I'll be waiting for you."

Five minutes later I was leaving, locking my front door behind me. When I turned around, I saw a group of reporters swarming around my house. They kept asking questions and shoving their microphones in my face. I pushed past them and ran to my car. Jumping in, I could hear their footsteps running after me. I locked the car doors and started the engine while they were knocking on the window asking more questions. I could hear the sound of my tires screeching as I drove off, leaving them standing there. I began to feel sick again but fought back the urge.

Chapter 2

Bearer of Bad New

*W*hen I arrived at my mother's house, I got out of my car and ran to the front door. I rang the bell several times. I knew it was the housekeeper's day off, but it seemed like an eternity before mother came to the door

"Well, what a pleasant surprise, come in dear." Diana bent down to kiss her mother on the cheek. "I just finished cutting fresh roses from the garden and was arranging them in the entry way vase."

"Where is dad," I asked. "He went to the bank to catch up on some paper work." I reached for my mother's hand as I said, "Mother, please sit down; I have some terrible news." She looked up at me with raised eyebrows, "Diana, your scaring me," she said. I took a deep breath as we sat down on the sofa. "Mother it's Georgette." "What about Georgette," she said as she waited for my next words. "Mother, Georgette is dead and her head was mailed to me in a box."

"What!! Whatever are you talking about? There must be some mistake!" She jumped up from the sofa and after taking a few steps, she fell to the floor in a heap. She'd fainted.

"Mother! Mother." I began lightly slapping her cheek and calling her name repeatedly, she finally started to come around. I could see the confusion on her face as if she were trying to determine if she had really heard the fate of her eldest daughter, or was it all just a dream?

I was finally able to get her up from the floor. After putting her left arm around my shoulder, I put my right arm around her waist as I guided her back to the sofa and sat her down. "Mother are you alright?" "Yes, I think so. Did you just tell me Georgette died?" "Yes mother, Georgette is gone." The tears began to flow down her cheeks. I reached for a tissue on the table and handed it to her and then I reached for another, as my own tears began to flow. I held her as we both sat crying for Georgette.

"When? How did this happen?" "I don't know, I'm just as mystified as you are. Would you like me to go by the bank to tell Dad or do you want to tell him?"

She thought for a moment and then decided, "I think it would be better if I wait until he gets home, I'll tell him then." I asked if she were sure and she replied, "Yes, I'm sure." I didn't want to leave my mother alone, but she insisted she would be fine and so I kissed her goodbye and left, promising to check on her later in the day.

Chapter 3

Pondering the Message

*C*ynthia, was standing outside pacing back and forth on the porch when I arrived. I could see the concern written all over her face. She didn't wait for me to get out of the car before she came hurrying down the front steps to meet me.

"Di, what in the Sam Hill is going on?" She often used this euphemism in place of the word 'hell'. (Although my government name is Diana, Cynthia has always called me Di).

I started crying and wiping my runny nose again as I exited the car. "Cynthia, you won't believe what just happened. I still can't believe it myself." We walked up the front steps together, both of us waiting to get inside before another word was spoken.

I entered the house behind Cynthia and sat at the kitchen counter. She came into the kitchen and reached for a fresh tissue and handed it to me as the one I was still holding was in shreds.

We had been besties since elementary school. We did everything together and told each other our deepest, darkest secrets. "What's going on girl?" Cynthia said again as she sat down beside me.

I told her everything that happened that morning while she sat there with a look of disbelief and shock, with her mouth wide open. Her first question to me was, "Why didn't I call her first?" That's when I realized that I hadn't called the police, they just suddenly showed up at my door. I told her, I didn't remember calling the police and didn't know how they knew to come to my house.

Cynthia made us some tea and we sat talking about what happened most of the afternoon. Although she and Georgette never liked each other much, she was very supportive and sympathetic, offering to go to the precinct with me the following day.

Later in the day, Cynthia ordered a pizza but when it was delivered, neither of us could eat a thing. She tried to get me to lie down and get some rest. I did lay down but sleep escaped me. I just kept going over and over in my head everything I could remember about the last time my sister and I spoke to each other. I didn't understand who would want to hurt Georgette or why?

I would drift off to sleep but would wake up sweating from one crazy dream after another. Finally, daylight came and I was anxious to shower and get dressed. When I got out of the shower, I could smell coffee brewing and bacon cooking. My stomach still felt a little queasy and the smell of that bacon didn't help my physical condition at all.

"Good morning," Cynthia said as she entered the bedroom carrying a tray filled with bacon, eggs, a croissant, strawberries, orange juice and coffee.

"Thanks girl, I wish you hadn't gone through all that trouble. I still don't feel like eating anything." "Oh no, you need to try to eat something." She said as she placed the tray on the bed. "O.K., I'll try." She smiled and told me not to worry, that she was going to shower, dress and go with me.

I felt a little relieved, as I didn't want to go alone anyway. I picked up the orange juice from the tray and took a few swigs along with two Tylenol that I retrieved from my purse, hoping it would help the headache that was gnawing at me.

Cynthia and I were finally ready and we left her house together. I was still very curious to find out how the police knew to show up at my house. Did someone hear me screaming and call? I didn't know.

Traffic seemed to be worse than usual that morning but we finally arrived at the precinct. After driving around for another 10 minutes, we were able to pull into a space just as another driver pulled out.

After we were parked, Cynthia grabbed my hand and said, "Let's pray before we go in there." We held hands and she led us in a prayer, asking the Lord for his protection, comfort, peace, safety, wisdom and clarity of mind. I didn't know what to expect but nevertheless, I was anxious to get started.

We went in together. I reached in my purse and pulled out the business card that was given to me the previous day. Looking around I saw an officer sitting behind a desk. The nameplate on the desk said Desk Sergeant. I walked up to the desk and waited for him to notice me. After a few minutes he looked up and said, "What can I do for you?" I told him my name and asked to speak to Detective Lance Griffin. (That was the name on the business card that was handed to me the previous day).

The Desk Sergeant took the card from my hand as he got up from his chair. He walked into one of the cubicles. After a few minutes he returned and said, "Follow me please."

Cynthia and I began to walk behind the officer. He turned and looked at her and said, "Not you. You can have a seat over there, please." Cynthia sighed and turned to walk over to the bench the officer pointed out to her. She sat down and our eyes met. She had a look of concern on her face. I mouthed the silent words "It's okay" and smiled as I turned to continue following the officer, who by now was a good 15 feet ahead of me.

The officer led me to a room marked interrogation. He opened the door and waited for me to walk through. He told me to have a seat and Detective Griffin would be with me shortly. I sat down. The room had two chairs and a small table.

It was about 20 minutes before the detective appeared with a big smile on his face. He apologized for keeping me waiting. He asked if I wanted something to drink and I declined.

I wanted to get straight to the point and before he could ask me anything, I said, "Sir I was wondering who called you to come to my home yesterday?" He looked at me puzzled and said, "Called me, why no one called me. I received a letter with no return address. When I opened it, your address was printed across the top. Below the address was a message.

"Message? What message," I said. He opened the folder that he brought into the room with him and pulled out a sheet of bond paper that had been folded and stapled to an envelope. He handed me the page, I began to read the message.

> "Bludgeoned in the head Killed her dead!
> Her face etched with pain.
> Nothing ventured, nothing gained.
> Drama driven trauma.
> I wonder, who's to blame?"

A large lump began to rise up in my throat as I read and reread the message. The officer spoke before I was able to grasp what I had just read. "Of course we were concerned that a possible murder may have taken place at your address or something.
That's why I came."

He asked me many questions about Georgette. He wanted to know about her lifestyle, if she had a boyfriend, when had I talked to her last, did she seem bothered or agitated lately. What was our relationship like, were we close, did I know of anyone who would want to hurt her? On and on for hours. Finally he said I could go but I should not leave the city. My eyebrows raised.

"Why?" I asked. "Am I a suspect?" He smiled again and said they had to consider all those who were closest to the victim. He told me to let him know if I thought of anything that may be of help to them in solving this case, no matter how minuscule it may seem.

I said I would. I stood to leave and my legs seemed to buckle under me. Detective Griffin caught me before I went down and asked if I was alright. I said I was and this time I was able to walk toward the door unassisted.

When I got to the outer office, Cynthia was curled up on the bench asleep. I nudged her and she woke up. "What time is it?" I told her it was 3:00 p.m. She said, "You were in there for a long time." I nodded and said, "Come on, let's get out of here." We left and walked out into the hot afternoon sun.

After we got settled in the car, Cynthia wanted to know everything. I told her all that had taken place in the interview and she listened quietly as I talked.

We stopped at a café nearby as I was feeling a little faint and weak because I had not eaten any solid food since very early the day before. Although I was still not hungry, I realized my body needed some nourishment.

Chapter 4

The Wakefield's

*D*iana's father and mother, Jonathan and Wilma Wakefield had been married for about two years when Georgette was born.

Her family was considered to be self-made. They were financially affluent and politically influential.

Her mother met her father, when he was just 23 years old. He was fresh out of college and had just started working at the only bank in town which happened to be owned by none-other than his father, Jonathan Wakefield Sr.

The story Diana had always been told was that her dad was immediately smitten with her mother from the very first time he laid eyes on her. It was the day she came walking into the bank to open up an account. He courted her mother vigorously by showering her with poetic words of love and gifts.

Jonathan's mother, looked down on his chosen love interest. She discerned something evil lurked within her and she did and said everything possible to keep the two of them apart. Nevertheless, Diana's father would not be dissuaded. The more they talked against Wilma, the more he wanted her.

In spite of Jonathan's mother's disapproval, the two slipped away one weekend and eloped. Grandma Wakefield was furious when she found out. She never forgave her son for his choice for a bride and for cheating her out of the grandiose wedding she always visualized for him.

Grandpa Wakefield on the other hand, was a very mild mannered man and kept quiet about the matter. No one really knew his views on the situation until he had a sudden heart attack and died at the bank one morning while sitting at his desk drinking coffee.

When Grandpa Wakefield's Will and Testament was read, everyone was shocked to find out that he had left the bank to his only son, Jonathan, Jr.

He left the house and some property to Grandma Wakefield who immediately fainted after the Will was read.

Diana's father was a very hard working man, often burning the candle at both ends. I guess he wanted to prove that he was worthy of the position that he had inherited.

The following year after her father became president and bank owner, her mother became pregnant again and Diana Wakefield entered the world nine months later. She became the focus of Grandma Wakefield's affections.

Georgette felt the sting of being cast to the side once Diana was born. In retaliation, she became rebellious and unruly. Her behavior earned her the title of being known as the black sheep of the family. It seemed like all of the family was pretty much in agreement on that issue. With Grandma Wakefield as their primary influence, many of the family members turned their noses up at the mere mention of Georgette's name.

Georgette was like a chameleon, turning into the very distasteful things that had been prophesied over her life by various family members.

Georgette and Diana were very close in the early years. Diana loved her sister very much but as they got older she did not agree with Georgette's lifestyle and thought she could shame her into being a different person. Since Georgette was older, Diana would always tell her that she should be setting a better example for her. She would often talk down to her in a very offensive manner. She felt like many of the other family members, that Georgette was an embarrassment to the family and to the community.

Instead of trying to encourage and build her up, Diana would degrade her and tear her down. She was as guilty as the rest. She thought her evil words would make Georgette change her ways. Instead, they only made her sink deeper into destructive activities.

Georgette was ostracized and eliminated from family reunions and other functions because the family disliked her behavior. She seemed to always be involved with men of questionable character. There were whispers of her having secret affairs with married men among other illicit behavior patterns.

The Wakefield's lived in a small town where everybody knew everybody. Everybody also knew everybody else's business and

Georgette had much unsavory business to know. In spite of Georgette's treatment, she didn't seem to be phased by it all and continued to live her life just as she pleased.

She had become very secretive in the last few weeks before her disappearance, exuding a quiet radiance that was unidentifiable. When Diana asked her what was going on with her, she would smile and say, "Oh nothing, nothing at all."

Chapter 5

Baffling Piece of Evidence

*C*ynthia and Diana sat talking at the Café long after the waitress cleared their table. At least she had managed to get down half of her vegetable omelet before asking the waitress for the check. Cynthia picked up the check from the table, "I got this." "No I got it, you've done enough for me already." "Don't be silly, that's what friends are for."

Laying the check back down on the table, she reached into her purse, pulled out her wallet and placed the needed cash in the little card holder. Then she laid a tip on the table and put the salt shaker on top of it. "Thanks girl." I really appreciate you," Diana said smiling as she grabbed Cynthia's hand.

Cynthia was in agreement that Diana should stay with her until the police finished at her house. The detective told Diana it would be at least a few days.

Diana still couldn't believe it. Georgette was gone. She felt like she was watching a movie and although this terrible tragedy had taken place, she was unable to fathom the magnitude of it all. Who would do such a terrible thing and why?

She racked her brain over and over to see if there was some detail or something out of the ordinary about her sister in the last few months, but everything about Georgette was out of the ordinary.

They stood up to leave and the waitress came over to the table, thanking them as she gave them a big smile.

They walked to the car and Cynthia drove them back to her place. Neither of them talked much on the way back. Diana was exhausted and her body was sore from the tenseness she felt. She just wanted to sleep.

Cynthia literally took care of her. They both called their bosses and asked for time off.

Later on Cynthia tried to get Diana to eat a bowl of homemade chicken soup she'd made, but Diana still wasn't hungry and only managed a few sips of the broth before putting the spoon down.

She took a sleep aide in order to get some much needed rest. She tried not to think about Georgette's head in that box but it kept coming back to haunt her over and over again.

After Diana had been at Cynthia's for three days, Detective Griffin called her on her cell phone. "Hello, Ms. Wakefield?" "Yes." "This is Detective Griffin." "Yes?" "I was wondering if I could have a chat with you this morning. That is, if you are available to come down to the station? I have a few more questions to ask you." "Yes, I'll be there."

Cynthia had to go into work that day and Diana would be alone anyway. She needed a distraction as her nerves were getting the best of her. After a hot shower and some clean clothes, Diana felt a little better as she had not been out of her pajamas in two days and was unable to get herself motivated.

Traffic was heavy and Diana was feeling antsy, wondering what Detective Griffin wanted to talk to her about. She couldn't imagine any other questions he could have. After all, he'd grilled her pretty good that first time.

After riding around the block several times, finally there was someone coming out of a parking space and she was able to ease into it as soon as the other driver pulled out. Diana wasn't one to pray much, but just before she got out of the car, she felt this strong urge to pray. Sitting there with her head bowed she said, "Lord, I need you more than ever. I've been a wreck since this tragedy occurred. Please help me to assist the police in any way I can. Amen."

She jumped out of the car, pressed the button on the key fob to lock the doors and started across the street. She took a deep breath before entering the building. The same Desk Sergeant was on duty, looking up he asked if he could help her. "Yes, I'm

Diana Wakefield, I'm here to see Detective Griffin." He stood and said, "Right this way please. The detective is waiting for you."

Diana followed him to the same little interrogation room. He told her to have a seat, the detective would be with her shortly. It seemed like an eternity before the detective finally entered the room. Again he had a folder in his hands. "Ms. Wakefield, I'm so sorry to keep you waiting."

"There has been a new development in your sister's case." Diana looked at the detective expectantly. "You found the rest of her body?" "Well not exactly, not yet anyway," he stated. "What is it then?"

"The coroner found a message rolled up in a small Ziploc bag with a rubber band wrapped around it and lodged in the back of your sister's mouth.

Diana asked what the message said and he looked down at his notes as he began to read:

> "Covered in water, branded
> at the heart, this is how I've
> hidden the very next part."

Afterward, he looked up at Diana, "Any idea what this means?" She sat for a minute pondering the contents of what the detective had just read to her. "Anything at all?" The detective waited for her reply.

She could think of nothing significant. It was mystifying to say the least. However, she wanted an opportunity to ponder it some more later. She pulled out her cell phone and typed the message on her notes page so she wouldn't forget it.

Suddenly, Diana remembered that she and Georgette use to play along the river bank when they were kids… but it seemed so farfetched that she hesitated to mention it.

"Well, it probably doesn't mean anything, but my sister and I used to play along the river bank behind the town church many years ago.

"Okay, is that it? Does anything else come to mind?" "No, no nothing." "Okay Ma'am, thank you for coming in.

"Is that all?" "Yes Ma'am, for the time being; that's all. I'll have the Desk Sergeant to escort you out."

As he reached for the door knob he turned and said, "By the way, you can return to your home now. We having finished there and we are sorry for any inconvenience our investigation has caused you." Diana thanked him as he opened the door. Turning to her once more he said, "Oh, one more thing," "I know detective, don't leave town," she said. He smiled as the Desk Sergeant appeared at the door and escorted her out.

Chapter 6

Pondering the Puzzle

*D*iana left the precinct with the message still on her mind. She couldn't help but think *of the callousness it took to murder someone, cut their body up, and proceed to play a game that provided clues that would lead to the retrieval of the body parts. Who does that?*

As she started the engine of her car, she dialed Cynthia's work number on her cell phone. She answered on the second ring. "Baker & Baker Associates, this is Cynthia, how may I help you?" "Hey girl, have you been to lunch yet?"

"No, I was just about to go, why?"

"I just left the precinct. That detective called and asked me to come in again. He said he had some more questions to ask me. How about I meet you at that little health food place down the street from your building in about 10 minutes? I'm not too far from you."

"Okay, I'll see you there," Cynthia said.

Diana maneuvered her way through the lunch hour traffic to the health food restaurant. She could hardly wait to share this latest development with Cynthia. She was hoping between the two of them; they could come up with some ideas that would be helpful in leading the detective to the place where the rest of Georgette's body was hidden.

Thank goodness the restaurant had a parking lot adjacent to their building as parking downtown was always a challenge.
She turned in the lot and took the first available space.

Diana could see Cynthia from the window as she walked to the entrance. They locked eyes and waved at each other. She came through the front door and made a beeline toward the table. Cynthia said, "I hope you don't mind, but I took the liberty to order for you. It will save time as it gets crowded in here and they only have one waitress working today."

"That's okay. You won't believe this latest development in Georgette's case. It seems the medical examiner found a piece of paper rolled up in a small plastic bag and lodged inside of Georgette's mouth."

"What! What did it say?" Diana said, "It had a message written on it. Hold on, I put it in my notes page on my phone. Here it is." Diana read the message aloud to Cynthia. "How intriguing!" "What do you think it means?"

By this time the waitress was standing at their table holding two identical plates of food, some of which Diana didn't recognize. "Can I get you anything else?" Diana asked her for a glass of lemon water and Cynthia said she would have the same. The waitress retreated across the room and went behind the counter to get their drinks.

Cynthia was looking over the message again, she said, "This looks like some kind of clue that should lead the police to the rest of Georgette's body."

They talked about it throughout the lunch hour. Nothing significant seemed to come to mind that they thought would help solve the case of who killed and dismembered Georgette or what had become of the rest of her body.

Diana reminded Cynthia that they use to throw rocks along the river bank, down by the church years ago on their way home from school. However, they weren't able to ascertain what the other verse meant regarding being branded at the heart. It didn't make any sense.

Cynthia, looked at her watch just about the time the waitress was walking by. "May I have the check please?" The waitress stopped and tore off the top copy of her pad and left it on the table. Diana picked up the check and they began to gather up their purses.

Heading toward the register, Cynthia thanked Diana for picking up the check. "That's the least I can do."

She told Cynthia she would be going back home that night, although she wasn't looking forward to it. Cynthia had made Diana feel very much at home during her short stay and said there was no hurry for her to leave. She told Diana she could stay with her as long as she needed to. Nonetheless, she knew she couldn't stay at Cynthia's place forever and decided it was time to go home.

Back at Cynthia's, Diana started gathering her things together. She wanted to be gone

before Cynthia got home from work.
Otherwise, she knew Cynthia would try talking
her into staying longer. Besides, she needed
more time alone to think, to focus.

Diana also felt very strongly that the
message had another hidden meaning that was
yet to be discovered. Lately, her mind and
emotions were all over the place. She just felt
like being alone.

Chapter 7

Studying the Messages

*D*iana turned the key in the lock and walked into the house. It smelled musty. She began opening up windows and spraying air freshener in all the rooms.

Her eyes caught a glimpse of the phone light blinking to indicate she had voice messages. Picking up the phone, she pressed the button to listen to her messages. The first one was from her mother. She sounded worried, "Hi Diana, its Mom. Please call me when you get this message." The next two messages were from her mother also. They pretty much said the same thing.

Diana dialed her mother back. She wondered why she hadn't tried calling on her cell phone. Her phone rang several times and on the third ring her voice recorder came on with her usual bubbly greeting, "Hi, you have reached the Wakefield residents. Please leave us a message and we will return your call as soon as possible. Have a great day."

Diana left her mother a message. "Hello Mother, it's me. I got your messages. Call me back when you can." She put the phone back in the cradle and walked over to the kitchen counter where she'd left her purse, keys and cell phone. She decided to try dialing her mother's cell phone.

Wilma, picked up on the second ring. "Diana, where are you?" "Hello Mother, I'm home right now. I just walked in a few minutes ago. I forgot to tell you I was going to be staying at Cynthia's for a few days." "Baby, I was worried." "I know, I'm sorry. Why didn't you call me on my cell?"

Frustrated, Wilma said; "I would have except, I don't know your cell number by heart and I couldn't find my cell phone at the time to look it up in my contacts."

Wilma was forever losing her cell phone. Diana said, "What's up?" "I was just wondering what was going on? Have you heard anything more about your sister?" "As a matter of fact, I have. I was just at the precinct again this morning. The Detective working the case asked me to come in again. He said he had more questions." "Oh, what kind of questions?"

"I'll come by a little later and tell you all about it." "Well I'm at the beauty salon right now and then I have bridge club afterward."

"Okay, how about I come over in the morning for coffee and tell you all about it?" "Okay Dear, I'll see you then."

Diana was a bit relieved her mother wasn't available that day. She really needed more time to try and sort things out in her mind.

She, clicked on her cell phone notes page and began to look over both messages again. The print was a little small. She went down the hall to her bedroom to get her reading glasses from the nightstand. Plopping down on the bed, she began studying the two messages again. Diana was hoping it would help her to understand more fully what the messages meant. Still, nothing new really jumped out at her.

She kept thinking about how they played along the river bank, when they were kids. The thought continued to nag at her brain.

Diana reached over to pick up the phone, then put it back down in the cradle and went to the kitchen to get the detective's card out of her purse. She just kept thinking the river bank down by the church had something to do with it. It seemed like such a small thing, but it was all she had.

She dialed the number on the card and the detective picked up right away. "Detective Griffin speaking." "This is Diana Wakefield."

"Oh yes Ms. Wakefield, how can I help you?" "I know this may sound a little strange, but I keep getting this feeling that the river bank in back of the town church has something to do with this case. I know it sounds far-fetched, but I just can't seem to get the thought out of my head."

"It's strange that you should mention that Ma'am as I haven't been able to get it out of my head either. In fact, I was thinking of having some divers to go in the water tomorrow at that very location, just to put my mind at ease about it."

"Really?" "Sure, I mean, it's just a hunch but what else do we have to go on?"

The detective said he would let her know if anything turned up. Diana thanked him and hung up. For some reason, she felt excited as if something were about to happen.

She read over the messages once more. After yawning several times, she took her charger out of the drawer and connected the plug to the wall socket and the other end to her cell phone. She laid the cell phone down on the nightstand, scooted down flat and pulled up the throw she had at the foot of the bed to cover herself. Minutes later, she'd drifted off into a deep sleep.

Chapter 8

Branded Arms

*D*arwin, the church handyman was driving along Highway 76. It had a feeder road that led into town. He sang as the volume of his voice matched the capacity of the country western music he had come to love so much. The sun was shining for the first time in a solid week. Everything seemed to be sparkling clean as there had been a daily barrage of pouring down rain. Finally, there was not a cloud in the sky and the weather forecast boasted a high of 78 degrees.

He pulled up his Ford F150 behind the town church as he always did and hopped out, after taking a sip from his piping hot coffee cup. He was in a good mood for a change. Darwin climbed the few steps of the church as he reached for his keys to unlock the back door. Putting his key into the lock he realized someone had not only left the door unlocked, it was also left ajar. *Hmmm, that's strange,* he thought. He was sure he had locked it when he left the church two nights ago. He worked at the church three days a week, doing odd jobs like keeping the carpets vacuumed, dusting the pews, filling the convertible baptismal pool with water and draining the water after every use. He also did minor repairs and kept the church grounds nicely manicured. He trimmed the trees as needed. Bulbs were planted late in Autumn and flowers in the Spring and Summer.

He would set the sprinkler system to water as needed, depending upon the weather. He decided to leave the sprinklers off as the ground was still very soggy from all the rain that had taken place throughout the week.

The pastor always left Darwin a note that was attached to the cork board in the entry way just off the kitchen. It would apprise him when the pool needed to be filled or emptied. Taking another sip from his coffee cup, he went straight to the board. As always, there was a note on the board held there by a push pin. He stood there reading the note that asked if he would please empty the baptismal pool. (A few new members had gotten baptized during the Wednesday night Bible study). It also had various other chores listed for him to complete.

He took a long swig from the large coffee cup, emptying the last few drops and crushing the cup in his hands before throwing the empty container into the trash that was just inside the kitchen door. Turning, he walked swiftly toward the utility closet to get the hose. Darwin knew that it took a while to empty the pool and if he started it first, he could get the vacuuming and dusting done before the pool would be empty.

He grabbed the hose off the hook and proceeded to pull one end of the hose out the back door where the water from the pool would drain. He pulled the other end of the hose down the hall to the sanctuary. He drug the hose over to the baptismal pool, screwed it into the water drainage pipe and turned the water release valve on.

Darwin went back down the hall to the back door to make sure the pool water was draining properly, it was. He turned his attention to the utility closet again. Taking out the vacuum cleaner and duster, he started toward the sanctuary. He plugged the vacuum cleaner in the wall and started the arduous chore of vacuuming the sanctuary carpet. After he finished, he removed the plug from the wall and began to wrap the cord around the device and proceeded to roll it against the wall.

Now it was time to dust the pews. Darwin was very meticulous about his work and took great care to make sure he had dusted every area of the sanctuary. When he was finished, he took the duster and the vacuum cleaner and rolled it down the hallway toward the utility closet.

He then turned toward the back door, checking to see if the water was still draining from the hose outside. It wasn't. He began checking to see if there was a kink in the hose, there wasn't. He looked at his wrist watch. He knew it normally wasn't finished draining yet. It should have taken at least another 30 minutes.

Feeling somewhat agitated, Darwin decided to go back into the sanctuary and take the lid off the baptismal to see if the pastor's washcloth had been left in the pool by accident. He always used a clean white washcloth to hold over the candidate's nose just before submerging him or her into the water. Sometimes it was left inside the pool which ultimately covered the drain and kept the water from escaping.

The top was heavy and would require him to use both hands to remove the lid. He sat the lid upright against the wall. Looking into the water, something inside of the cavity blocking the drain caught his eye and it wasn't a washcloth.

At first, he squinted to get a better look and then his eyes widened in disbelief as he jumped back. Turning to run, he tripped over the hose as he ran screaming down the church aisle and out the front door.

The police found Darwin leaning against the church fence outside. At his feet was a huge splattering of the breakfast he had consumed that morning at the diner before he came to work.

One of the officers walked up to Darwin and asked if he had called 9-1-1. He shook his head up and down as he blew his nose with a handkerchief from his back pocket. He then pointed to the church and said to the officer, "In there." The officer raced up the church steps with his hand on his weapon. He took his gun out of the holster and cautiously walked inside. A few minutes later he came outside again. He was speaking into his walkie-talkie. Walking over to Darwin again, he asked him if he was alright. The officer then went over to his car and opened the door on the driver's side, he reached into the console and took something out. He closed the car door and walked back over to Darwin, handing him a mint he said, "Here suck on this, it will help to settle your stomach."

Several police cars were pulling up to the church and officers were jumping out of their vehicles to converse with the first officer on the scene. They all went into the church and walked toward the baptismal pool. As they looked over, there lying at the bottom of the pool was the upper half of a female body.

The arms were crossed in front of the body. The left arm had a tattoo of a heart in the upper left quadrant of the arm. Inside the tattoo was a cross that had been seared into the skin with what appeared to be a branding iron of sorts. The hands were missing.

When the police came outside of the church, a black unmarked car drove up and stopped. Turning off the engine, a young handsome man stepped out of the vehicle. It was Detective Griffin. He walked inside the church and after a time he returned, pulling a tablet from his inside jacket pocket as he walked over to Darwin. He was still leaning against the fence looking as white as a ghost.

"Hi, I'm Detective Griffin and you are?" "Darwin, Darwin McGhee."

"Can you tell me what happened here?" Darwin began telling the detective all that had taken place since he arrived. "Is there anything else you can think of, anything at all?" Darwin thought for a moment and then a light bulb seemed to come on in his head.
He said, "Yes, as a matter of fact, when I got here this morning, I noticed the

backdoor was unlocked and slightly ajar.
I thought it was strange. Although the
backdoor is open at times, it has never
been left ajar.

The detective was writing in his tablet. He
looked up and asked Darwin if he knew
whether anyone else had a key to the back door.
Darwin said the pastor had a key and the
pastor's son, Marcus had a key. There was also
a key left on a hook in the utility closet. He
wasn't sure who else might have one.

The detective reached in his pocket and gave
Darwin a business card. "If you think of
anything else, even the smallest detail; please
give me a call. Darwin said he would and the
detective turned and walked back toward the
church. Halfway up the steps he turned to
Darwin and asked if he knew where the pastor
was? Darwin told him that he didn't know, that
he hardly ever came to the church on Friday's.
He asked him if he had the pastor's cell phone
number. Darwin pulled out his cell phone from

his back pocket and began scrolling through his contacts until he came across the pastor's cell phone number. He gave the detective the number and the detective wrote it down in the tablet and put the tablet in his inside jacket pocket. Then turning he continued up the church steps. As he reached for the door, he turned once again toward Darwin and said, "You can go now, but don't leave town, I may have more questions for you later."

"What! Am I a suspect? I swear, I don't know where that body part came from, you gotta believe me. I just work here part time, three days a week doing odd jobs." "Calm down young man, this is just routine questioning. You understand, don't you?"

"Oh okay," Darwin said. He walked over to his truck, got in and drove off.

Chapter 9

Intrigued

*D*etective Griffin, pulled out his cell phone as he entered the sanctuary. He dialed a number and someone on the other end answered.

"Yeah Grady, do me a favor and cancel the divers for this afternoon, I believe we have found what we were looking for." He listened and then he said, "Thanks." Putting the cell phone back in his pocket, Detective Griffin made a mental note to call Diana Wakefield when he had a chance.

Diana pulled in front of her mother's driveway the next morning. She didn't worry about blocking in her dad's car in the garage. She knew he always left very early every morning and it was already 8:15 a.m.

She reached in her purse and pulled out a bottle of eye drops and squeezed two drops of the liquid in each eye. Diana had been crying and she'd hoped to keep her eyes from looking red and puffy.

She'd had an emotional morning thinking about her sister, Georgette and blaming herself for being so judgmental and downright unkind to her at times.

Diana jumped out of the car and walked to the front door. She rang once and within a few seconds Nancy, the Wakefield housekeeper was at the front door. She opened the door with a big smile on her face. "Good morning Ms. Diana, your mother is on the patio."

"Thanks Nancy," she said over her shoulder as she walked through the foyer, into the living room area and out the French doors to the patio. There, her mother sat looking radiant as always. Diana leaned over to kiss her cheek. "Good morning, Mother." "Good morning Darling. I was just about to call you." "I told you I would be here early." "I know, but I was very restless last night. I wasn't able to sleep at all. I was up, showered and dressed before your father left this morning. I don't understand why I'm getting second hand information anyway. Why doesn't that detective call me? After all, I am Georgette's mother. You would think that counts for something." "Now Mother, I'm sure he doesn't mean anything by it. He probably assumes I am keeping you informed, and I am."

Wilma sighed and with a wave of her hand she said, "Enough of that, tell me what is going on with the investigation?" Diana leaned in and looked around as she wanted to make sure Nancy was not within earshot.

"Mother, you won't believe this, but the coroner found a folded paper wrapped in a small plastic baggy that was rolled up, secured with a rubber band and wedged in the back of Georgette's mouth." Her mother leaned forward with her eyes wide, "What! What paper? What did it say?"

"It was a message. I've put it in my cell phone notes page. Diana reached in her purse for her phone. She began reading it softly as her eyes darted back and forth between the phone, the French doors and then at her mother.

Diana's mother's eyes were now wide open and so was her mouth. "Let me see that." She snatched the phone from Diana's hand, picked up her reading glasses that were right next to her plate and put them on.

"What kind of nonsense is this and what in the world does it mean?" "That's what the detective was inquiring about. He wanted to know if I had any idea what it meant. I told him I didn't."

"This must be some kind of sick joke," her mother retorted. "That's not all," Diana said, "the detective called me this morning on my cell phone when I was driving over here. He told me that they found the upper portion of a female body with the arms folded in front. It was found at the church inside of the baptismal pool." Wilma gasped! "Is it Georgette's body?" "They don't know just yet. He did say the coloring of the arms looked the same to him as the head of Georgette. He asked me if she had a tattoo of a heart on her upper left arm and I told him she did."

"This is all so disheartening. I'm just so terribly distraught! Diana's mother began to sob uncontrollably. "Why would someone do such a thing and what does it all mean?" "Don't cry Mother." Tears began to stream down Diana's face as well. She hated seeing her mother in such turmoil. She had tried to hold it all together but once her mother began crying, Diana couldn't contain herself any longer."

Nancy suddenly came through the French doors. "Is everything alright Mrs.?" "Yes, I'm fine Nancy, you can clear the table. I've suddenly lost my appetite."

"Yes Ma'am," she said as she began clearing the dishes from the table. No one spoke until the table was cleared, wiped clean and Nancy had disappeared inside of the French doors again. Then Diana leaned over and whispered, "The detective wants me to meet him at the coroner's office this morning to see if I can identify the tattoo on the upper left arm as Georgette's.

Wilma jumped up and said, "I'm going with you." "Mother, I don't think that's a good idea." "Diana, I'm going and that settles it! I have every right to be there." "Okay Mother, you're right. I'll drive and bring you back afterward." "Thank you, dear."

Diana paced back and forth in the foyer as her mother got her purse. She started toward the front entrance when Nancy came running behind her with her cell phone. "Mrs. your cell phone." "Oh thank you Nancy, I should be back in a few hours." "Yes, Ma'am."

Diana drove in silence. She wanted to give her mother a chance to regain her composure as she seemed very distressed and Diana didn't want to say anything that may further upset her.

They arrived at the coroner's office 20 minutes later. She parked and they both exited the vehicle.

Diana and her mother walked arm and arm up to the entrance of the building. They walked inside and went right up to the information desk. The lady at the desk looked up and asked if she could help them. Diana said, "Yes, I'm Diana Wakefield. Can you direct me to the coroner's office?" "Yes Ma'am it's down this hallway, the last door on your left. Please sign the log for me." She handed Diana the clipboard that had a pen attached to it. She signed in for herself and her mother. Thanking the attendant, she handed the clipboard back to her. They proceeded down the hallway. At the end of the hall on the left side was a door marked City Coroner. Diana turned the knob. The door was locked. There was a sign next to the door that read, please ring the bell for admittance. She rang the bell and shortly afterward the door was opened by a short stocky gentleman with a bald head wearing spectacles.

Diana spoke first. "Hello my name is Diana Wakefield and this is my mother, Wilma Wakefield. We are supposed to meet Detective Griffin here."

"Yes, he is waiting for you, come right this way." He escorted the two ladies into another room where the detective was waiting, "There you are," he said. "I'm so sorry to keep you waiting detective. This is my mother, Wilma Wakefield. Mother, this is Detective Griffin." The detective looked Wilma over and nodded his head. "How do you do Ma'am?"

Wilma nodded, "As well as can be expected." The room was small and had a glass window. On the other side of the window was a table on wheels that was covered with a white cloth. There was a young man standing at the table looking out at them. The detective looked at him and nodded his head. The young man rolled the table over to the window and removed the cloth that covered it. Wilma gasped!

Suddenly, Diana could feel the weight of her mother's body pressing against her. She held on to her and asked if she were alright, Wilma replied, "Yes."

Detective Griffin looked at Diana and asked if she recognized the tattoo on the upper quadrant of the left arm. Diana said she did. It was the same one she'd seen on Georgette's arm.

The detective nodded at the attendant again and he pulled the sheet over the body part and rolled it away.

The detective directed both ladies to the chairs that were placed up against the wall on the other side of the small room. "Let's sit down over here." They sat down and he sat between them as he rummaged inside of his jacket pocket. "By the way, I got the message right here that I was telling you about over the phone." He pulled out a small plastic bag that had a folded piece of paper inside and tape on the ends. "The coroner found this taped to the underside of one of the arms. It's another message. He handed it to Diana's mother and she proceeded to remove the message from the bag and unfold it. Reading it out loud, she said:

"The lower half was thrown out like trash on the street called Chambers.

She'd walked right into danger!
I wonder, was it just a stranger?
No one seems to know. The Saga continues to grow."

The detective took the message from Mrs. Wakefield, folded it and placed it carefully back inside the bag and put it back in his jacket pocket.

He stood as if to dismiss them. "I just wanted to keep you up to speed on what we'd found. Thank you both for your time."

"Detective do you have any leads yet?" "Well actually Ma'am, we are still trying to piece this all together and hopefully find the rest of your daughter's body. We'll keep you informed. So long ladies." He turned and walked out of the room.

Chapter 10

Cynthia Dupree

*C*ynthia woke up with a splitting headache. She wanted to call her boss and request a sick day but she had already been warned that she was taking too many days off. She dismissed the idea. The last thing she needed was to be fired due to attendance. She needed that job desperately.

She dragged herself up from the bed, slipped on her robe and headed to the kitchen to make a cup of coffee. She sat her cup under the spout of the Keurig and put a Folger's decaf pod inside. While she waited for the water to boil, she reached into the cabinet over the microwave and found the bottle of Tylenol. Putting two in her mouth, she then opened the refrigerator door and got a bottle of water to wash them down.

Picking up her coffee, she headed to the bathroom to shower and get ready. By the time she was ready to go, her headache had subsided.

The alarm on her phone was going off. She always set it every night for early morning to remind her to check her calendar to see what was on her agenda for that day.

Opening up the calendar to the current date she saw her notation to go by the nursing home to see her mother. It was just a few blocks from her work and she decided she would go on her lunch break instead of after work. Traffic was a bear on Friday's after 3:00 p.m. and she didn't feel like dealing with it.

Gulping down the last few drops of coffee, she grabbed her keys, purse and the bottle of water that was still sitting on the kitchen counter. She turned off the lights and walked out of the front door, locking it behind her. She took a deep breath as she tried to prepare her mind for the day ahead.

Cynthia stepped off the elevator and walked down the hall to her office. She could hear the phone ringing before she made it to the door. Running to her desk and dropping her purse in the drawer with one hand as she reached for the phone with the other. "Baker & Baker Associates, this is Cynthia."

She listened patiently as the lady on the other end of the phone began ranting and raving about the bill she had received from the law firm. Cynthia apologized to the caller and asked her to hold while she transferred her to the billing department.

Her morning was spent typing court documents. When she looked at her watch, it was 12:30 p.m.

She transferred her calls to the answering service, grabbed her purse from the drawer, and left the office.

The elevator was full, there was just enough room for her to squeeze in. After the doors closed the occupants descended to the lobby in silence.

When Cynthia arrived at the nursing home, she rang the doorbell. They kept the door locked as some of the patients were known for wandering off the premises unaccompanied. She was peering through the glass doors and could see the attendant behind the desk look up. Recognition showed on his face as he reached for the buzzer to let her in.

"Hi, Mr. Martin," she said as she passed the front desk. "Hello, Ms. Dupree," he replied. Cynthia proceeded down the hall. Her mother's room was at the very end. The door was pulled to, but not completely closed. She knocked and pushed the door open. Her mother peered at her from the bed where she was propped up.

"Hi Mom." She bent down to kiss her mother on the forehead. "How are you doing today?"

"Shhhhhhh!! Judge Jada is on," her mother replied.

Cynthia knew what that meant. When Judge Jada was on, her mother was fully engrossed in the television and would not initiate conversation or respond to conversation directed toward her until a commercial came on.

Suddenly, there came a breaking news story across the TV screen, interrupting her mother's most coveted show. The newscaster was talking about a serial killer who had been killing and dismembering women. He had been spotted within 60 miles of their town.

Cynthia was amazed by the mere thought of a serial killer being so near the town where they lived. During the news broadcast, her mother finally looked over at Cynthia who was sitting in the chair near the bed checking her cell phone messages.

She finally decides it was a good time to engage her daughter in conversation. "How are you today, dear?"

"I'm okay. I just wanted to stop by to see my favorite girl. What's going on with you?" Her mother says, "I was just about to make dinner for your father, I'm cooking his favorite today, smothered chicken with rice, gravy and fresh string beans."

Cynthia's dad had died five years ago from cancer. When he was alive, he would come home from the small corner store he managed at about 1:00 p.m. in the afternoon to have his heaviest meal of the day. In the evening, her mother would fix him a light supper which usually consisted of soup and salad.

Her mother had begun having these imaginary occurrences more frequently due to her Alzheimer's condition. She would imagine she was cooking for her husband or pressing his work shirts. Cynthia never corrected her. The doctor had previously explained to her that often people with Alzheimer's can lose track of dates, seasons and the passage of time. Sometimes they may forget where they are or how they got there.

Cynthia somehow felt like she would be taking away the last remnants of happiness from her mother if she attempted to erase the images from her mind, of a time when she was very happy and had the love of her life still present with her as her husband was for over 60 years.

Changes in her mother's behavior began to happen several years after her father's death. She knew she had to do something on the day her mother forgot she was cooking bacon on the stove and almost burned the house down.

It hadn't been easy since her father passed. The nursing home was costly and Cynthia barely made enough money to scrape by now that she had the responsibility of caring for her mother placed squarely on her shoulders.

Most of her father's retirement money had been squandered away due to some bad investments he made late in his life. Her parent's house had several liens against it for unpaid debts. She was still paying off those debts so that she could satisfy the liens and sell their home. In addition, the kitchen had sustained extensive damage due to the fire caused by her mother. She was still working through the red tape with the insurance company to get that situation resolved. No one knew what Cynthia was going through, not even her best friend, Diana. She kept quiet about her financial troubles and had learned how to put on her game face whenever she was in the company of others. She believed somehow things would work out.

She hadn't been going to church as consistently as she once had. Largely due to her struggle to pay her tithe and offerings. Deep down inside, she felt like God had abandoned her. Cynthia, spent many nights releasing the silent tears that quietly streamed down her face and fell repeatedly on her pillow.

Checking her watch again, she stood, kissed her mother goodbye and told her she would be back to see her in a few days. Her mother nodded as she watched the last few minutes of Judge Jada.

Chapter 11

Wilma's Warning

*W*ilma was rather shaken when she left the coroner's office but she was very careful to mask her emotions while she was in the company of Diana. She didn't want her daughter to ask questions.

She kept quiet and began looking out of the window as if she were engrossed with the view. Diana kept glancing at her and after a time she asked, "Are you okay Mom?" "Yes dear, why do you ask?" "Oh nothing, you just seem like you're far away. I wondered how you were holding up in light of these most recent events."

Wilma sighed, "To be honest, it is most unsettling to say the least and to make matters worse, I don't have a clue what it all means." Diana patted her mother on the hand. "I'm sure the detective will be able to sort it all out in time."

Diana pulled into the driveway and opened her door to exit her car, her mother touched her arm and said, "No need to go in dear, I'm going to lay down for a while, I'm afraid this whole sordid affair has worn me out." "Okay, Mother." Diana leaned over and kissed her mother on the cheek. "I'll call and check on you later."

Wilma got out of the car and walked toward the front door. Diana waited for Nancy to come to the door. Once her mother was safely inside, she started backing out of the driveway.

Once inside, Wilma went upstairs to her bedroom. She kicked off her red bottom stiletto's and walked toward her closet to pull out her flat riding boots, a pair of black leggings, her black turtleneck sweater and her black and purple checkered cape. Then she reached up to the top shelf and grabbed her fedora hat.

It was time to pay Pastor Dillion a visit. She left the clothing she had taken off sprawled across her bed. Walking down the front staircase of the house, she called out to Nancy to please hang up her things. "Yes Mrs.," Nancy said as Wilma went out the garage door to her car.

Wilma called Pastor Dillion and let him know she was on her way to the church. She asked him to leave the back door open for her.

"What's this all about," he said. "I'll tell you when I get there." She hung up and continued toward the town church. When she arrived, she began looking around nervously. No one seemed to be about. Wilma pulled her fedora down over her eyes as she drove her car around to the back of the church.

She got out of the car and climbed the back steps. Taking one more look around and seeing no one, she grabbed the door knob and turned it. The door creaked as it opened and she walked inside.

The pastor was waiting for her and ushered her into his office where he closed the door behind them. "Hello David," she said. Ignoring her greeting, he retorted,

"What's going on Wilma?" She began telling him all that had taken place since the story broke in the newspaper of Georgette's head being delivered by mail to Diana's house.

The police were playing this one very close to the chest. They made sure no updates about the case were leaked to the press. The detective's boss had made it clear that if anything got out about the investigation, there would be hell to pay.

He turned pale as he reached for a glass of water. "Who do you think is behind this?" "I don't know, Wilma said. "I wondered if the police had questioned you and if so, what did you tell them?"

"I told them I was at home when my handyman found partial remains of a human body in our baptismal pool. I told them I didn't have any idea who the partial body belonged to or why someone would put it in the pool."

Wilma leaned over his desk, whispering she asked, "Do you think they believed you?" "I, I think so, but I'm not one hundred percent sure. Don't worry, I was very careful not to give anything away with my answers. Remember, I have just as much at stake here as you do. I am the pastor of this church as well as a married man. The last thing I need, is for my reputation to be tarnished. I have a congregation of members, a wife and a son who would be devastated if they knew I had fathered an illegitimate child, even though our brief encounter happened a long time ago."

Wilma nodded her head as she rose to leave. "See to it that you keep it that way, I have never told a living soul that you are Georgette's father. I want your assurance you will take that secret to your grave. Never reveal it, no matter what! We both have too much to lose." With that, Wilma opened the door and left without another word.

As Wilma walked down the hallway toward the back door, she thought she heard a noise. She stopped and turned around, seeing no one; she opened the door and went out.

Chapter 12

Painful Memories

*P*astor Dillion sat at his desk long after Wilma Wakefield had gone. Staring blankly into space as his mind drifted back to the painful memory of that fateful night 28 years ago.

He had only been pastoring at the town church for a little over a year. His wife, Bethany was uncomfortable being a pastor's wife. She had shared her concerns with him before he accepted the position of pastor that had been offered to him by the church's board.

Bethany felt they would be constantly under a microscope and she was not sure she was able to measure up to the expectations or the isolation that often came with the title of first lady. She had been saved at a very young age and was always very observant of the position of first lady. At least in her church back home, the first lady of their church was never at any functions that went on outside of the church. There would be baby showers, bridal showers, blessings of new homes, luncheons for this occasion or that occasion.

Bethany was always acutely aware of the first lady's absence from such events. She wondered why no one ever addressed the elephant in the room. She wasn't sure if an invitation had been extended or the first lady had just chosen not to attend these functions. Nevertheless, she concluded that the position of first lady must be a very lonely one.

Being an outgoing person, Bethany didn't want the stigma of being labeled an outsider within her own church family. She was very apprehensive about her husband accepting this position that would take them into uncharted territory. After all, David had not pastored a church before. However, after much prayer;

they agreed that it was God's will and so they gathered their courage and forged ahead.

As soon as they arrived and began to settle into the town church, Bethany began hosting tea parties for the ladies. She started a Christian book club and busied herself with visiting the sick and shut in. She was also involved in all sorts of charitable events.

Their son, Marcus had not been born yet and she did not want to stay at home alone and risk being thought of as untouchable. In fact, she was gone so much that David hardly ever saw her until she came to bed at night. Usually, by that time he had already tired of waiting up for her and drifted off to sleep. There intimate time together suffered and they eventually became somewhat estranged.

On Sunday mornings during church and Wednesday nights during bible study they appeared to be the perfect couple. But behind closed doors, nothing could be further from the truth. He had talked to her many times about spending more time at home but she wouldn't hear of it. They had even argued about it a few times. As a result, David became very aloof which made Bethany throw herself into being 'church busy' all the more.

There was even a women's prison in a town about two hours away. Bethany and a team of three other members would go to that prison once a month to minister to the inmates. They would have dinner afterward and then make the two hour drive back to town.

On one particular occasion, it poured down raining a good portion of the day and was expected to continue raining throughout the night. David was worried about Bethany and the team of other ladies driving back. He called her and suggested they stay overnight at the hotel in that town and put the charges on the church's credit card. They were able to double up and get two rooms with two double beds in each room to accommodate the four of them.

It was early evening but it was already dark outside and David was not up to going out in the rain. He remembered there was leftover chicken in the refrigerator from an event Bethany hosted the previous day. He decided to make a sandwich and brush up on his sermon for the next day.

He was eating his sandwich when he heard the front door of the church slam shut. Someone had come into the sanctuary crying. He got up from his desk to go see who it was and if he could be of assistance. Lying on the altar stairs, drenched from head to toe was none other than Wilma Wakefield. "Sister Wakefield, oh my goodness! You are soaked" As she continued to ball her eyes out, Pastor Dillion took her by the hand and drew her up. He took off his jacket and put it around her shoulders as he walked her into his office. Sitting her down on the office sofa, he told her to wait right there and he would get some dry towels.

When he returned with the towels she was still crying. He gave her the towels and told her to dry herself off while he went to the kitchen to make her a hot cup of tea.

When Pastor Dillion returned, he was holding a tray that had a small teapot, a cup and saucer, a bowl of sugar and a creamer filled with half and half. Turning his back to the door he pushed it gently with his foot and backed in holding the tray with both hands.

When he turned around, Wilma was standing in front of his desk. Her hair was still dripping wet. The towels the pastor had brought to her earlier, draped her body. He saw her clothing on the floor in a heap beside her. She was no longer crying. She began to speak, "I'm so lonely, he never comes home until very late at night and then he falls into bed and sleeps like a baby while I lay there burning with desire for him." The tears began to stream down her face again. "I don't think he finds me attractive anymore. Do you think I'm attractive Pastor?"

She loosened the grip on the towels, allowing them to slide to the floor. There she stood in all her glory, naked as a jaybird! She began walking toward him. Once she was close, he could smell her intoxicating fragrance.

David was frozen. His eyes were big as saucers. He could feel the blood rushing to his head as she took the tray from him and sat it down on the small table near his desk. His mouth was dry as he watched her close the distance between the two of them. Wilma put her arms around his neck and pulled him close, sealing his lips with a deep and hungry kiss. He tried to push her away. Everything in him wanted to turn and run, but his knees were weak. She slid her tongue into his mouth and from that point on, he was doomed!

He began to respond to her advances and before he knew it they were on the sofa making passionate love to one another.

Afterward, they rose in silence. David pulled his pants up and Wilma gathered her wet clothes from the floor. She was about to put them back on wet when he took them from her and told her he would put them in the dryer that was just down the hall next to the utility room. He left his office, walking down the hall to the area where they washed the church's towels and table clothes. He threw the clothes in the drier and stood there for 15 minutes waiting for them to dry. When he came back with the dry clothes, Wilma was sipping on the tea with the towel wrapped around her. She put the cup down and dressed in silence.

Once she was fully clothed, she tried to kiss him on the forehead, but he turned away. Wilma sighed. She then turned and left his office. She walked through the sanctuary and out the front door of the church into the cold, dark, and wet night.

Pastor Dillion walked into the sanctuary as tears welled up in his eyes. He was overwhelmed with the magnitude of what had just taken place. Falling on his knees at the altar, he cried out to God, "Lord, please forgive me! I have sinned before you." His tears came in huge drops, rolling down both cheeks. He banged his fist on the floor and wept until there were no more tears. He lay there for quite some time before he was able to pull himself up and leave the church.

As the months went by, Wilma continued to attend church as if nothing happened. Pastor Dillion found it extremely difficult to preach with her staring at him from the congregation.

It was his custom to go to the back of the church after the benediction to shake hands and give hugs to his members as they left the sanctuary. On one particular occasion, when he reached out his hand to shake Wilma's hand, she gave him her hand and he felt a note being pressed into his palm. She let go of his hand and he slipped the note in his pocket.

After everyone had gone, he went into his office. Closing the door behind him, he reached into his pocket to retrieve the note Wilma had slipped him. When he opened the note it said, "Congratulations, you're going to be a daddy." Next to it was a smiley face.

The sudden loud ringing of the desk phone jolted him back to reality. He picked up the receiver, "Hello Pastor Dillion speaking."

Chapter 13

The Secret

*J*onathan Wakefield Jr. was a man that rose very early in the morning. He would shave, shower and dress for work. By 6:00 a.m. he was sitting down to breakfast. The morning newspaper would be beside his plate. Nancy would have already poured his coffee and the unmistakable smell of bacon would be permeating throughout the air.

He would take that first sip from his cup and after he felt it slide down his throat into his stomach, he would pick up the newspaper to check the stock market page to see whether the Dow Jones average was up or down that day.

Jonathan was a man of few words and because of this characteristic, he was often mistaken for someone who was very passive.

He often observed his surroundings with quiet dignity. His feathers were not easily ruffled.

When he married Wilma, he made it his business to do all he could to ensure his success. Although he loved her very deeply, he could see that she was very materialistic and thrived on his undivided attention. It was tough in those earlier years when he was struggling to make his bank account match his wife's spending. He would easily put in 15 or 16 hours a day at the bank.

When she became pregnant with Georgette, he had only been intimate with her once or twice during that entire month. Nevertheless, he didn't question it, as it is possible to become pregnant with only one encounter. He was delighted that she was expecting their first child.

He knew he had not spent as much time with her as he should have in the past. Things at the bank were starting to improve to the point that he felt comfortable coming home earlier to be with her. She was so happy, he vowed he would not neglect her again if he could help it.

Although the baby was born a month earlier than Wilma's projected due date, he thought she had somehow miscalculated. The baby was healthy and didn't need to be incubated as most premature babies do. When Jonathan questioned the doctor he said, "Although it is the exception and not the rule, some women continue to have their cycle for a time after becoming pregnant. The doctor's explanation satisfied Jonathan for the moment.

As the months went by, Grandma Wakefield would come by to see her first grandchild. She often made comments to Jonathan whenever Wilma was not within earshot, that Georgette looked nothing like him or Wilma. There was also the issue of the possible miscalculation of the delivery date.

She began to pressure Jonathan to get a DNA test. However, he refused.

One Saturday when Wilma needed to go out, she asked her mother-in-law if she would watch Georgette. Grandma Wakefield's original thought was to decline the offer, but before the words were out of her mouth, she reconsidered and decided to accept Wilma's offer to babysit. She thought to herself, w*hat a great opportunity to swab the inside of Georgette's mouth with a Q-tip and place it inside of a Ziploc bag. She would then try again to entice Jonathan to mail the swab to the DNA laboratory in the next town for testing.*

Later that day, after Grandma Wakefield came over, she showed the swab to Jonathan and pleaded with him to mail it off. "If you don't mail it off for testing, I will!"

Jonathan wasn't sure he even wanted to know. He and Wilma were very happy during that time and he didn't want to find out something that he would regret. Besides if

Wilma ever found out what they had done, she would be furious!

Nevertheless after much prodding from his mother, who was finally able to wear him down; Jonathan agreed to swab his own mouth and send both Q-tips for testing.

As soon as the package was mailed, he immediately regretted it. He found himself anxious and moody while he waited for the results to come back. It took about six weeks before he received the results. He had the results sent to the bank as he didn't want to risk Wilma intercepting the mail.

Thankfully, the day the results came in the mail, Jonathan's secretary was out sick. He picked up the mail that was left in her inbox by the mailroom clerk and began to skim through the different envelopes. Suddenly he came across one envelop that had the return address of the DNA clinic he mailed the swab to. He

took that letter out of the stack and headed to
his office. Once inside, he locked the door. His
hands were shaking as he retrieved the letter
opener from his desk and slit the flap from one
end to the other. He removed the letter from the
envelope and unfolded it, reading its contents
twice. The results stated Jonathan was not
Georgette's father.

That evening Jonathan came home much
later than usual. Wilma was sitting in the living
room when he arrived. She jumped up
screaming, "Where have you been? I've been
worried sick. Why didn't you call me?"
Jonathan walked right past her and went
straight to the bar to pour himself a drink. He
drank it down in one gulp. He never looked at
Wilma or said a single word.

Wilma, ran over to him and began beating
his chest with her fist. "How dare you! You
reek of alcohol." Still, Jonathan was silent as he

poured another drink and drank that one in one gulp as well.

Wilma knocked the bottle of Hennessey on the floor and it shattered in many pieces. She was livid and began calling him names.
"You are a poor excuse of a man. You're weak, cold and insensitive! I don't know why I put up with you!"

Turning toward her, Jonathan spoke for the first time, "My dear, you put up with me for the money, the prestige and the luxuries that come with being my wife." He staggered toward the staircase. Before climbing the stairs, he paused and looked at her with his pointer finger wagging he said, "No worries though, it will all balance out in the end."

Wilma, told him in no uncertain terms where he could go. As Jonathan was climbing the stairs, he turned once more and said, "You first!"

That was by far the worse argument they had ever engaged in. Jonathan was angry with Wilma for cheating on him and then lying about Georgette being his child. He was also angry with himself that he didn't have the guts to leave her.

Wilma completed him, she was full of fire and very charismatic, not to mention he was captivated by her beauty. He wanted to punish her severely. He was heartbroken. Yet, at the same time; he loved her so much that part of him couldn't bear the thought of losing her.

The next morning Jonathan skipped his usual leisurely breakfast and left for work before Wilma was awake. He'd stored the DNA results in his safe deposit box at the bank the day before.

He wanted to punish Wilma for cheating on him and deceiving him. He wanted to get revenge and still remain married to her. He suddenly got a brainstorm and a huge smile came across his face.

That day, he called his mother and told her that he'd gotten the DNA results back from the lab. He lied, telling her the results confirmed he was Georgette's father.

He knew his mother would never have accepted that child as part of the Wakefield family if she knew the truth.

Nevertheless, Grandma Wakefield remained suspicious. She wanted to see the results for herself but Jonathan told her he destroyed them so that Wilma would not find out. He cautioned her not to question the validity of Georgette's birthright again.

From time to time, Grandma Wakefield would babysit but she never really got close to Georgette. After Diana came along, it was obvious to anyone who paid attention, Diana was her favorite and she constantly lavished that child with affection.

One day, Georgette asked her mother, "How come Grandma Wakefield doesn't love me?" Wilma would hug her and say, "Don't be silly Georgette, of course she loves you."

Whenever Georgette and Grandma Wakefield were alone, the opportunity was never missed to tell Georgette she was a bad seed. Her grandmother disliked her intensely and would always call her "evil." Eventually, as Georgette got older, she began to act like the various negative labels that had been attached to her.

Down through the years, whenever they had family gatherings, other family members would observe Georgette's bad behavior and began talking to one another about what a horrible child she was. They started declining invitations to attend these functions if they knew Georgette would be present. Needless to say, she became an outcast. Although it hurt her deeply, she pretended like she was not bothered by the cold shoulder treatment she received from her relatives.

Ultimately, Grandma Wakefield passed away, but the label of disgrace she'd initiated toward Georgette remained and continued to influence the point of view adopted in the minds of the Wakefield family.

Chapter 14

Marcus Dillion

*M*arcus was Pastor David Dillion's only son. He was tall, dark and very handsome. He had hazel eyes that sparkled and the prettiest set of pearly white teeth you ever saw.

However, Marcus seemed oblivious to his good looks. Generally he could be found with his head in some intellectual book or other. He was also known as a mathematical genius around town.

During his high school years, Marcus made his extra money tutoring those who were not as astute in Math as he was. He graduated from high school and went to a small community college in a nearby big city where he obtained his Associate's degree.

The pastor worked a second job until Marcus graduated as things were financially lean.

Afterward, Marcus was able to get a full scholarship to Stanford University where he earned a Bachelor's and a Master's degree in Accounting, graduating with honors.

Marcus wanted to join an accounting firm in one of the big cities, but the pastor persuaded him to come back home and work at the church as accountant. Marcus felt he owed his parents that much for all the sacrifices they had made for him. Reluctantly, he returned home.

Pastor Dillion, trusted Marcus and felt very comfortable putting the church's finances in his hands. The church's bookkeeping system needed to be updated. After settling back into small town life again, Marcus rolled up his sleeves and started looking over the church's finances and proceeded to get the books in order. He had some ideas that he discussed with his father that proved to help the church get back on its feet. Within a few years, the membership grew and the church's financial status improved greatly. Marcus was very proud of the huge accomplishments he'd made working beside his father in ministry.

Cynthia was a regular at church and she'd had her eye on Marcus for some time. After all, she was still a young girl in her 20's and was very lonely. Cynthia decided to change her hairstyle and although a new wardrobe was definitely not in her budget, she went to the local boutique and tried on at least a dozen outfits. She had managed to stay in pretty good shape, keeping her weight under control by running three miles, four days a week.

All of the outfits she tried on looked great on her. The sales clerk could tell she liked everything, but seemed hesitant about making the purchases. She suggested that Cynthia use their layaway plan. This idea seemed to help her to make the decision to use that option to update her wardrobe.

After several months of making payments, Cynthia was excited about finally being able to take her new wardrobe home.

She couldn't wait to walk into church the next Sunday morning. She knew she was looking drop dead gorgeous. She'd hoped her attempts to get Marcus' attention would finally pay off. However, he seemed preoccupied and didn't notice her at all. Cynthia was crushed. She was at a loss for what to do next.

While thinking about what she might do to gain his attention, she had an idea. "I know," she said, after snapping her fingers. Since Marcus was the accountant for the church, she decided to deviate from her normal habit of putting a few dollars in the offering plate. Instead, she would write a check the following Sunday. Only she would conveniently forget to sign it. Surely he would call her when he saw the unsigned check and ask her to come by the church to sign it. She laid back on her bed with her arms folded behind her head. She was feeling proud of herself that she had come up with such a great plan.

The following Sunday, Cynthia couldn't wait to implement her strategy. She had her check filled out before she got there, with the exception of the signature. Later as the offering plate passed in front of her, she placed the check in the basket.

Monday, Cynthia waited expectantly for Marcus' call. She had an anxious feeling in the pit of her stomach all day. By the end of the day, he had not called. Disappointment gripped her as she walked to her car, after leaving work that day.

Suppose he doesn't call at all? What then, she thought. She didn't want to think about that possibility. Maybe he hadn't had an opportunity to look at the checks from the offering yet. That night, she couldn't stop thinking about it. She tossed and turned most of the night. When the alarm went off, she reached over and hit the snooze button. She had only slept a few hours and wasn't ready to get up yet. The alarm sounded again and Cynthia tried to drown out the annoying sound by putting her pillow over her head.

However, she wasn't able to go back to sleep. She turned off the alarm and threw back the covers "Alright, alright I'm up!"

After brushing her teeth, she showered quickly and dried off. She sat in the chair at her dressing table and picked up the bottle of lotion and began smoothing it all over her body. She put deodorant under her arms and sprayed on her favorite perfume. Standing up, she walked over to her closet and let her eyes slowing peruse through the rack trying to decide what to wear. She settled on her pale pink and burgundy paisley dress and her cream colored pumps.

Cynthia had barely gotten to her office before the phones started ringing off the hook. She was extremely busy all day. When it was time to go, she realized she had not heard from Marcus. *Surely he has come across that check by now*, she thought. She turned out the light and locked the office door behind her.

When Cynthia arrived home, she parked her car and got out. Just before running up the stairs, she stopped to check the mail. There were two envelopes, one was her electric bill and the other was a letter sized envelope with the church's return address in the upper left hand corner. Cynthia held her breath as she opened it. Inside was her unsigned check with a small yellow sticky note attached. It simply said, "Please sign and return." At first, Cynthia was furious, but then she thought; *I know, I'll sign it and take it by the church tomorrow, during my lunch hour.* She vowed, she would make him notice her if it was the last thing she did.

The following day, Cynthia could hardly wait until lunch time came. She spent most of the morning trying to think of something clever to say when she saw Marcus but found herself dismissing every possibility. As soon as it was 12 o'clock, she grabbed her jacket from the back of the chair and got her purse out of the desk drawer. She left her office and drove to the church. She decided she would stop at the church altar in the sanctuary and say a prayer before walking back to Marcus' office.

Cynthia kneeled down in front of the church altar. Before she knew it, she was pouring her heart out to God about her loneliness, her crush on a man who didn't even know she was alive and her financial situation due to the monthly bill that had to be paid to the nursing home. She got up from the altar feeling a little better and walked toward the door that leads to the church's administrative offices.

The pastor's office was at the front of the hallway and Marcus' office was near the back. She could hear voices coming from the pastor's office. She started to tiptoe by, but a familiar voice stopped her in her tracks. It was the unmistakable voice of none other than her best friend's mother, Wilma Wakefield.

Cynthia paused briefly to listen. What she heard, almost made her gasp out loud. Wilma Wakefield was talking to Pastor Dillion. She heard her say, "See to it that you keep it that way, I have never told a living soul that you are Georgette's father. I want your assurance you will take that secret to your grave. Never reveal it. No matter what! We both have too much to lose."

Cynthia's mouth was wide open. She covered her mouth with her hand to keep any sound from escaping from her lips. Her eyes were as big as saucers. She couldn't believe what she had just heard. She started to back up as Wilma's voice sounded like it was now closer to the door. She was looking around for a place to hide, when she saw the small alcove just behind her. As soon as she darted into the alcove and pressed her back up against the wall, Wilma opened the pastor's office door, closed it quietly behind her and walked hurriedly down the hallway towards the back entrance of the church.

Cynthia stood there for several minutes. She was in shock regarding what she had just heard. Her idea to go to Marcus' office under the pretense that she had only come to bring him a signed check, suddenly went out the window.

A better plan was beginning to formulate in her mind. It was an offer she knew he wouldn't be able to refuse. It would have to wait until another day when her plan had taken its full shape. She quietly tiptoed back to the sanctuary entrance and retreated out the front doors.

Chapter 15

Counsel

*I*t was Friday night. Diana walked in the door, kicked off her shoes and threw her keys on the kitchen counter. She was exhausted. Lately she was keeping herself busy at the bank. She had been working 10 to 12 hour days. It helped her to keep her mind off the case. It also helped her to sleep better at night, especially after a hot bath and a large glass of chilled wine.

She hadn't heard from Detective Griffin in several weeks and made a mental note to call him the following day to inquire about the status of the case.

Although she was hungry and would have liked a home cooked meal, it was late and she was too tired to cook. She grabbed two slices of pizza from the fridge left over from the day before, heated them up in the microwave and scarfed them both down.

Afterward, she poured a large goblet of her favorite sweet red wine from the wine chiller and headed to the bathroom to turn on the tub faucet.

Diana sat the glass down on the bathroom counter. She opened the cabinet door under the sink and grabbed a bath bomb. After removing the wrapper, she dropped it in the tub and watched it fizz as it started to disintegrate. The water was frothy and began to turn a pale lavender color. As she was sitting on the side of the tub, she started to swirl the water around and around with her left hand. It felt soft and silky. The flowery fragrance from the bomb began to saturate the air.

She undressed and grabbed the glass of wine from the counter. After taking a big swig, she sat it down on the side of the tub and stepped into the water. It was very hot but she liked it that way. It took a few minutes before she was able to fully immerse herself. Finally, she slide down until only her head was above the water. Diana leaned back against the tub and closed her eyes. It felt wonderful and her body began to relax. She stayed that way until the water temperature started to change from hot to lukewarm.

Grabbing her luffa sponge, she washed away the grime from the day's activities. After repeatedly washing over her body with the sponge, she picked up the wine from the ledge of the tub and took another long swig.
By this time, she was completely relaxed. She rinsed the soap off herself and pulled the plug to let the water run out. Standing up, she reached for her towel on the rack behind her as she stepped out, using the towel to dry herself.

Afterward, Diana wrapped the towel around her upper body and picked up her glass from the tub's ledge. She walked barefoot into the bedroom and sat her glass on the nightstand. Closing the distance to the dresser, she pulled the drawer open and removed a fresh nightgown from the drawer. Unfolding it, she pulled it over her head and crawled into bed. She drained the remaining remnants of wine from the glass, turned off the light and scooted herself down between the covers. She slept soundly throughout the night.

Diana was awakened by the sound of her house phone ringing loudly. Without opening her eyes, she reached for the phone. After a few missed attempts, her hand found its target and picked up the receiver. "Hello." "Good morning Ms. Wakefield, This is Detective Griffin. I hope I didn't wake you, but there is a new development in your sister's case." Diana sat up abruptly in the bed, "What time is it?"

"Well, it's about 10:30 Ma'am. I was wondering if I might drop by today?" "What is it, Detective?" "Well I'd rather not say over the phone. I'll only need a few minutes of your time, say in about an hour?"

"Yes, yes of course." "Okay, I'll see you then, goodbye." "Goodbye, Detective."

Diana was dressed and barely had enough time to put the coffee on, when the doorbell rang. She went to the door and opened it, "Good morning Detective, come right in." "Good morning Ma'am." "Diana, please call me Diana." "Oh o.k., Ma'am, I mean Diana." "Would you like a cup of coffee? I was just about to have one."

"Yes, that would be nice," he said as he stood watching her."

After pouring two cups of coffee and putting the sugar and creamer on the counter, she noticed he was still standing. "Please Detective, sit down." He sat at the counter, picked up the cup she had poured for him and began to drink from it. She looked at him and said, "I was going to call you today." "Why is that?" "Well, I hadn't heard anything and I just wondered if there were any new developments."

"Well, as a matter of fact there is. The lower half of a female's body was found in a dumpster over on Chambers Street. It was the same skin tone as the other parts that we've found."

"Please don't ask me to come to identify it. I just can't bear to do that today." "No Ma'am, I took a picture on my cell phone, would you please take a look and let me know if it looks familiar to you?" "Okay, I guess I could do that much."

The Detective showed Diana the picture from his phone. She couldn't be sure about the legs, but she knew without a doubt they were indeed Georgette's feet, she would recognize those toes anywhere. She use to always kid Georgette about having such a long big toe and the rest of the toes were short. "Yes, they are definitely Georgette's feet." Diana began to cry, she was upset with herself as she had not expected to become so emotional. The detective got up from his chair and came around the counter where she sat, he patted her on the back and apologized for upsetting her. "I'm okay," she said.

"There's one more thing Ma'am," "Diana, please call me Diana." There was a plastic bag taped to the bottom of the right foot, it had a folded paper in it." "Was it another message?" Yes Ma'am, Diana, it was."

The Detective pulled a clear bag from his pocket. He pushed the Ziploc over to the other side and opened the bag. As usual, there was a folded piece of paper inside. The detective seemed to be taking his time unfolding the message. Diana could hardly contain herself, she wanted to scream out, "Hurry up already!" Finally, he had the message opened. Clearing his throat, he began to read its contents aloud.

"As they say, 'How you like me now?'
Did my messages manage to mesmerize
or mystify you somehow?
The final clue sent by this thriller, points
A finger straight at the killer."

Diana found the silence in the room that followed this latest development to be rather uncomfortable. "Is there anything that comes to mind that will shed a light on the contents of this message?" "No, I'm afraid not," Diana said. "Okay, I won't take up any more of your time." He turned and walked out the front door.

Chapter 16

Painful Heartbreak

*M*arcus Dillion sat in his office staring out of the window. He half expected to see that beautiful vision of loveliness prancing around on the banks of the lake in her bare feet, as he so often had in the past. Her shoes were left beside the large rock near the water. She was tall and slim. He would watch her often with his powerful zoom lens camera.

On several occasions, he even snapped her picture. He knew it wasn't right but he was unable to resist the urge. She was so beautiful. He was mesmerized by her. The pictures he took showed the droplets of water as they lay on top of her smooth skin.

She would always pull her hair back into a tight ponytail and twist it in a bun at the nape of her neck.

He hadn't been himself since her death. His heart and his arms ached for her. He still couldn't believe she was gone. He loved everything about her. The smell of her hair, the intoxicating aroma of her skin. The golden brown hue of her body, her beautiful smile, her pearly white teeth and her large brown eyes and full lips.

He began to reminisce about how they met. He remembers that day vividly. He finally got the courage to come outside and walk down to the water's edge to greet her. He just stood there watching as she danced and pranced through the water. She was a bit surprised and embarrassed when she turned around to see him standing there with a huge grin on his face.

"Hi," he managed to utter. It felt like he could barely breathe as she began to walk toward him. "Hi," she said back, "I remember you, you're Marcus, right?" He nodded his head up and down. "You're the pastor's son, right?" Again he nodded. "You were graduating from high school when I was just a junior. Of course, you were a bit nerdy for my taste back then. But, not so much now." He blushed. By this time she was standing in front of him with her right hand extended, "I'm Georgette Wakefield." He took her hand and pumped it gently up and down.

"Pleased to meet you," Marcus replied. She walked over to the rock and began to put her shoes back on. He sat down on the rock and they started talking. Conversation came easy between the two of them.

He found himself looking for her about the same time every day. Some days she would be there, some days she wouldn't.

He remembered the feeling he had whenever she didn't come. He almost felt lost, empty. He also remembered the feeling he had when he would look out the window and see her there.

His heart felt like it was about to explode in his chest.

He found himself thinking back to the day he saw her dressed in shorts and a tee shirt. It was particularly hot that day and he watched her through the office window as she decided to get completely wet all over. Normally she only removed her shoes and allowed her feet and legs to get wet. This day, she actually swam in the lake. She went out pretty far and then swam back again. When she came up out of the water her tee shirt was clinging to every part of her upper body.

Again, Marcus took the camera from his desk drawer, zooming in close, he took pictures of her as she loosened the bun from the back of her head and shook her wet hair out as the curls cascaded down her shoulders. That day, he made up his mind he would ask her out.

He put the camera in his desk drawer and locked it. He was a nervous wreck. He decided to pray before taking the plunge. Marcus prayed for courage to ask her out but he also prayed for the acceptance of her answer if it was not in his favor.

He walked out of his office and down the hall. When he got to the back door of the church he reached for the doorknob, turned it and pulled the door open. He walked outside and was disappointed to see that Georgette was gone. That quick! He wanted to kick himself. He waited too long and missed the opportunity.

Marcus went back inside and down the hall again to his office. He unlocked the desk drawer, took the camera out and put it in his leather camera case. He didn't want to do anymore work that day and left the office to go home.

That night he tossed and turned. He was unable to sleep. He got up and went over to the table where he had left his camera case. He unzipped the leather case and took the camera out. He sat on the bed and began looking at all the pictures he had taken of Georgette. He promised himself he would not miss another opportunity to ask her out.

Marcus kept his promise and he and Georgette began a beautiful whirlwind courtship. They spent many hours together, laughing and talking and just enjoying each other's company.

After several months of dating, he had fallen head over heels in love with her and she also fell hard for him. Georgette had not allowed anyone to get close to her before, but she felt a special connection to Marcus.

On Christmas Eve, he asked her to marry him. To his delight, she said "Yes."

Chapter 17

Baffling Outcome

*I*t was the end of January and Marcus told Georgette of his idea to tell his parents about their engagement on Valentine's Day. She reluctantly agreed.

When Valentine's Day came, Georgette was a nervous wreck. She wanted to call the luncheon off that Marcus had arranged for them all. Her stomach was in knots. Nevertheless, she prepared herself for their lunch and hoped for the best.

She bought a red dress for the occasion and had her hair washed and set at the beauty salon that morning. They were to meet at a little Italian restaurant where she and Marcus had their first date.

He picked Georgette up at noon. She expected his parents to be in the car but they both had an early meeting and agreed to meet them at the restaurant at one o'clock.

Georgette was exceptionally quiet during the ride. Marcus sensed her nervousness and grabbed her hand. She looked at him and managed a faint smile. "Don't worry, they will love you, I know they will." "I hope so, Georgette replied."

When they arrived, Marcus parked the car in the restaurant parking lot. He got out and walked around the car to help Georgette out. She held on to his arm as they walked in. The restaurant was crowded and busy but Marcus had called ahead days ago and reserved a private room for them. He left his parents' names with the greeter and asked her to please escort them to the reserved room when they arrived.

Almost as soon as they sat down and started to look over the menu, Marcus' parents were ushered in by the greeter.

Marcus stood up and kissed his mother as she was seated across from him. He introduced Georgette. Mrs. Dillion took one look at her and said, "Why Marcus, she's absolutely stunning. Where in the world have you been hiding her?" Turning to face Georgette she said, "We are so glad to meet you dear."

"Thank you, I'm happy to meet you as well." Georgette started to relax until she observed Mrs. Dillion look over at Pastor Dillion with concern. "Why David, are you alright? You're as white as a sheet." He mumbled that he was fine and abruptly excused himself to go to the men's room.

Pastor Dillion paced back and forth in the men's bathroom. He wet some paper towels with cold water and began to pat his forehead with them. He felt faint. He recognized Georgette immediately as he had made it his business over the years to quietly check on her from a distance whenever he could. After all, she was his daughter. He thought to himself, *what in the world is she doing with Marcus?* He finally regained his composure and went back out to his seat.

After everyone ordered and the waiter left the table, Marcus grabbed Georgette's hand. "Mom, Dad, I have an announcement to make. His mother looked at him expectantly, "Well don't keep us waiting. What is it dear?" "Georgette and I are engaged to be married."

"Oh that's wonderful," his mother gushed. I'm so happy for you both."

Just before Marcus made his big announcement, Pastor Dillion had chosen that moment to take a sip of water from his glass. As soon as Marcus announced his engagement to Georgette, he choked on the water and began coughing and sputtering. After a time, he was able to recover. "Are you okay, dear?" Ignoring his wife's question of concern, he looked at Marcus and said, "You can't marry her." Mrs. Dillion, looked at him with a confused look on her face, "Why on earth not?" Pastor Dillion, jumped up from the table and threw his napkin down, "You just can't and that's all there is to it." He turned and as he walked toward the door, he looked back at his wife and said, "Bethany, I'll be in the car."

Mrs. Dillion, sat there with her mouth open, she was appalled at her husband's behavior and couldn't understand why he had reacted so harshly to the news.

Georgette, sat there as the tears began to roll down her face. Marcus put his arm around her as he apologized for his father's behavior.

Just then the waiter came in with a large tray and proceeded to place a platter of food in front of each person. He also placed Pastor Dillion's food at his place setting, not knowing he would not be returning.

The Valentine's Day lunch announcement was supposed to be a delightful surprise. Instead, it was met with a firm rejection from Marcus' father, and left his mother baffled by her husband's behavior, reducing Georgette to tears.

Under normal circumstances, the aroma and presentation of the Italian cuisine would have made their mouths water. However, the atmosphere in the room had changed drastically. No one was able to eat very much. The nervous but jubilant couples that entered that intimate backroom space, were now experiencing a cold chill in the atmosphere. Hardly a word was spoken between them.

They all skipped dessert and Marcus paid the bill as they prepared to leave.

Mrs. Dillion turned to Georgette and taking her hand, expressed her happiness in having met her. Georgette forced a half smile and nodded in agreement. She didn't trust herself to say a word. She was afraid the flood gates behind her eye lids would open again and she didn't want that to happen.

Just as they were leaving, Pastor Dillion opened the door. "Bethany, let's go!" He turned and walked back out to the car, leaving his wife to apologize for his behavior before making a hasty departure after him.

Once they were on the highway, driving back toward town, she turned to him and said, "David what on earth has gotten into you? You were downright rude back there." He continued driving with his lips pressed tightly together. "David?"

"I don't want to talk about it! That girl is not right for him." "But David, you were just saying not too long ago that Marcus was working too hard and had not allowed any time for a social life. Now that we know he not only has a social life, but has met a young lady and fallen in love, you are dead set against the relationship without even giving it a chance? That's not like you."

"Bethany, not another word!" They drove the rest of the way home in silence.

Pastor Dillion spent the rest of the day in his office at the church. He was visibly shaken. He knew he was acting out of character. However, he had to find a way to keep Marcus and Georgette from marrying. After all, they were brother and sister! This situation was the worst possible thing that could have happened. How in the world did he not know about it?

He stayed at the church until well past his normal bedtime. He could think of no plausible explanation to give to Bethany and wanted to make sure she would be asleep before he went home. He didn't know what, if anything he was going to tell her and wanted to avoid any conversation with her for now. He was relieved when he got home to find her asleep.

Pastor Dillion rose before the crack of dawn the next morning. He showered and dressed, skipping breakfast he hurried out the door. He still wasn't ready to give Bethany an explanation of his behavior regarding Marcus and Georgette's engagement.

Although he had begged the Lord's forgiveness over and over again, he was still plagued with bouts of guilt and depression off and on throughout the years. That fateful night he shared with Wilma Wakefield so many years ago caused him great sorrow. It was easy for him as a pastor to tell others how the Lord forgives and forgets. He just couldn't seem to grasp that concept for himself. He would do anything to erase that night. Anything!

Chapter 18

Blackmail

Cynthia was sitting in her living room. The television was on and her eyes were fixed on the screen but she was not paying attention to what was going on. She couldn't get the conversation she'd overheard outside of Pastor Dillion's office out of her mind.

She was still pondering how she could use this information to her advantage. She wondered if Marcus knew of his father's infidelity. She thought if she was going to ever get Marcus' attention, it was worth a shot to find out if he knew already. She decided she would have one more go of it. This time, she would go to Marcus' office and try to entice him into asking her out. He seemed so preoccupied with something (or someone) else. What, she did not know; but she was determined to find out.

If her efforts to win his affections didn't pan out, she planned to blackmail him with the information she knew. After all, if she couldn't have him, she would make it difficult for him to be happy with anyone else, (if there was someone else). She also needed the money to help pay for her mother's nursing home expenses. It was settled in her mind and she began thinking about her next move to put her plan into action.

The next day Cynthia, put on one of the new outfits she'd purchased from the boutique. Her hair and makeup were flawless. She went to work feeling confident that today would be some kind of turning point in her life.

Something inside of her kept saying, if she wanted to be successful in life, she would have to take what she wanted by any means necessary. She was not willing to go on lonely, lacking financially, and unhappy. She had to find a way to get what she wanted, and what she wanted was Marcus as her husband, a plan that would position her to be financially stable. It never occurred to her to include love in her plan. It was a plan that was solely focused on possessions. Right now she was barely able to make it from pay check to pay check with the extra expenses of taking care of her mother. She never dreamed her life would turn out this way. However, she was determined it was not going to stay this way if she could help it.

Cynthia felt impatient all morning and could barely wait for lunch time. She was sure of one thing. Today, would be the beginning of a relationship with the man she had chosen to ease her financial burdens and resolve her feeling of loneliness or the beginning of a scheme to blackmail him in order to pay off the debts that had been thrust upon her. One way or another, she would eliminate one or both of her problems.

Finally, she was able to take a lunch break. She forwarded her calls to the firm's answering service and grabbed her purse from the desk draw. Sighing she walked toward the door and left the office.

All the way over to the church, Cynthia kept going over her plan in her mind. So much so, that she almost ran a red light and had to put on the brakes at the last minute. She closed her eyes for a moment as she whispered to herself, "Okay girl, get it together. Regain your composure." The car behind her honked his horn and she realized the light had turned green.

Cynthia came back to reality and drove off. She finally arrived at the church and pulled into the parking lot. She got out of her vehicle and walked to the front entrance of the church. However, on second thought; she decided to walk around to the back of the church and try that door first, as she knew Marcus' office was closer to that end and she wanted to minimize the risk of running into Pastor Dillion.

Nervously looking around, she ran up the back steps and turned the door knob. The door opened and she walked in. She tiptoed to Marcus' office door and knocked softly. A masculine voice behind the door said, "Come in." Cynthia opened the office door. "Hi, Marcus." Looking up with raised eyebrows he said, "Cynthia, what brings you here?"

"Well, I got your correspondence along with my check in the mail. I thought I would sign it and bring it back in person. I do apologize for the oversight. I don't know how on earth I forgot to sign it."

"No problem, it happens. But you didn't have to come all this way. You could have dropped it in the mail or put it in the offering plate on Sunday, there was no hurry."

"To be honest, I did want to talk to you privately. You always seem so preoccupied, I thought perhaps it would be best if I came over."

"Okay," he said. Cynthia cleared her throat and took a deep breath before she spoke. "The truth of the matter is, I was wondering if we could go out some time. You know, get to know each other better. Perhaps dinner and a movie?"

"Are you asking me out?" After a brief hesitation she answered, "Uh yes, yes I am. I figured you are single and so am I, so why not?" She stood there feeling like an idiot, as she waited for him to answer.

After clearing his throat he said, "Actually, I'm seeing someone." "What? Who? Is it serious?"

"Yes, it is serious." Again, Cynthia said, "Who?"

She could see Marcus squirming but she stood her ground, waiting for him to answer. Finally he said, "Well I would really rather not say just yet. I mean we're engaged but we haven't announced it yet."

Cynthia, looked at him dumbfounded, "Engaged?" "Yes," Marcus answered. Cynthia was embarrassed and hurt, she knew she shouldn't ask but she couldn't help herself. "Oh, how long has this been going on?" Marcus was starting to squirm, "What difference does it make?" It's really not important."

She started to raise her voice, "What do you mean it's not important? It's important to me." At that point, Marcus stood up and put his pen down on the desk, Cynthia had struck a nerve in him. "What, I do is none of your business, now I think you should leave."

Cynthia, was angry now. "Just who the heck do you think you are anyway?" You think you're better than me? You think I'm not good enough for you or something?" Marcus, came around the desk, walked past her and opened the office door. "What I think, is that you should leave. Now!"

"Okay, okay, but before I go, I was wondering if you knew that your father, the good pastor has a bastard child? Did you know that?" Marcus looked at her and closed the door back. "Whatever are you talking about?"

Cynthia began to tell Marcus about the conversation she had overheard between his father and a woman, (for some reason she did not reveal the identity of the woman at the time), "Maybe your mother would be interested in knowing that little bit of information? Better still, maybe I'll go to the town newspaper and tell them what I know."

"I don't believe you! Get out of my office and don't come back." "I'll go, but if I don't have $50,000 wired to my bank account by Friday, this whole town will know about your father and his illegitimate child. I'll even throw in the name of the child, for free, no charge!!!"

"Where would I get that kind of money?" "Well, I don't know. A big shot, savvy accountant like yourself, should be able to figure it out."

She handed him a piece of paper from her pocket. She had hoped she wouldn't have to use it. It contained her typed bank account information. She turned and walked out of his office.

Marcus stood there in disbelief. He couldn't fathom what just happened. He didn't know whether Cynthia was telling the truth or not but one thing he did know, he didn't want that slanderous information to get out, true or not; he knew it would hurt the ministry his father had worked so hard to build. In addition, he didn't want his mother to be hurt by such gossip. He knew if she got wind of it, it would kill her.

If he took the money from one of the church accounts, his father would notice such a large withdrawal. Although he trusted Marcus to handle the church's finances, he was very hands on and always looked over the church accounts regularly to assure himself everything looked kosher.

Marcus decided he would go to the bank first thing in the morning and try to get a loan to pay Cynthia the fifty grand in exchange for her silence.

Chapter 19

Sweet Reprisal

*J*onathan was surprised to look up from his desk and see Marcus standing there holding his briefcase. Marcus had been directed to him as both loan officers were out that day. He rose and walked toward him with his hand outstretched and a smile on his face.

"Good morning Marcus, what brings you here, young man?" Marcus shook Jonathan's hand and said, "Good Morning Sir, may I sit down?" "Of course, please do." Jonathan closed the door and directed Marcus to the chair in front of his desk.

He came right to the point and told Jonathan the story he had made up about he and his father wanting to finance a mission trip to Africa. The money would be used for travel expenses, food, mosquito netting, books, shoes and clothing for the children. It would also support a small team of engineers who would be used to build a well large enough to supply a community with uncontaminated water for a particular region that had no clean water.

He stayed up most of the night typing up a proposal for this venture and thought it would surely get him the desired funds he needed to keep Cynthia's mouth shut. As a matter of fact, his proposal was so good he thought about going to his father with his idea. They could actually do such a mission trip. The church had enough money in its account to support such an effort without totally depleting its savings.

Jonathan, seemed to like the idea and told Marcus to give him a few days to look over the proposal and he would get back to him by official bank letter. Marcus left the bank feeling relieved. He felt like the meeting had gone well.

Jonathan however, had no intentions of allowing such a large loan to go through, even though Marcus' proposal was very thorough and it showed the church had enough collateral for a loan of that amount. Marcus was a brilliant accountant and the church's finances had never been in better shape since the young man had returned from college to handle his father's church affairs.

Nevertheless, he always had a suspicion that somehow Marcus' father and Wilma had something covert going on back in the day. He use to watch the way she looked at him in church and the way the Pastor would blush against his will. He had no intentions of being made a fool of. He was not about to grant the loan request. Not now, not ever!

He took a large rubber stamp from his drawer and stamped the loan application 'Disapproved' and walked into the outer office to put it in his secretary's in-box with a note for her to type up a denial letter to send to the church.

He felt vindicated. He was not quite sure from what, he just knew somehow he had made the right decision.

Chapter 20

The Big Cover up

*M*arcus was stunned when he opened the morning mail. It was a letter from the bank. It said they regretted to inform him that the loan he requested was denied. He couldn't believe his eyes. The church's finances were in good order and he had done a fine job with presenting his business proposal to the bank. He couldn't understand why he'd been turned down. The letter just said the bank was not able to extend such a large loan at this time.

He didn't know what he was going to do. Then it came to him, he could try embezzling small amounts at a time from one of the church's accounts. He felt bad about doing such a thing, but he had no choice. He just hoped Cynthia would agree to allow him to pay her in five thousand dollar increments over a period of ten months. If she refused, he would be in a terrible dilemma; having no other viable resources where he could get the money.

Marcus thought if he had the first five thousand dollar installment in cash instead of depositing it in Cynthia's bank account, she would be more likely to accept his offer. The lust of the eye would surely be enough fuel to motivate her to go along with Marcus' proposition once she saw the cash.

They made arrangements to meet at a little Café near the edge of town. Marcus, handed Cynthia the envelope under the table as he tried to explain the impossibility of being able to get her such a large sum all at once without his father becoming suspicious. She looked in the envelope and quickly counted the money. "No way! You have until Friday to get the rest or I'll go to the newspapers."

Chapter 21

True Confession

*P*astor Dillion hadn't had a decent night's sleep since his son announced his plans to marry Georgette at the restaurant. He spent long hours locked in his study either at home or his office at the church. Relations with Bethany were strained, to say the least. She didn't know what to make of it all.

David was miserable, both physically and emotionally. He'd developed a terrible head cold. In addition, after all these years, he still felt guilty and the feeling got worse as time went by. He had prayed and asked for God's forgiveness over and over again, yet he did not feel pardoned. Why couldn't he accept God's forgiveness for his sin for that fateful night? You would think after so many years he would be over it. However, it came back to haunt him over and over again.

After praying for forgiveness once again, he got up from his knees. This time, instinctively; David knew what he must do. He was going to arrange a meeting with Wilma. He wanted her to be the first to know that he had decided to go to Jonathan and confess his sin. Maybe then he could move on.

Somehow, he knew in his spirit, this was the right thing to do. David called Wilma on her cell phone. She was on her way to her usual hair appointment when the call came through. She pushed the button on the steering wheel to answer the call. "Well hello stranger, isn't this a pleasant surprise. What, pray tell do I owe the honor?"

"Hello Wilma, I uh, I need to see you. Can you come by the church later this evening?" "Okay, what's this all about?" "I really would rather not say over the phone, but it's a matter of grave importance to me." "Alright, I'll be there around seven. Is that too late?" "No, no that's fine."

Wilma got to the church just in time to see Marcus' car pull out of the church parking lot. He appeared to be engrossed in his own thoughts and she was thankful that he didn't seem to notice her driving up to the entrance of the parking lot with her turn signal on.

She parked, exited the car and looked around before running up to the back door. She expected David to be in his office, but saw the kitchen light was on when she entered the church. He was standing at the far end of the kitchen with his fingers spread out in front of him on the counter.

"Hello Wilma." "Is that all I get? How about a hug?" She started walking toward him with her arms outstretched. "No," he replied a little too vehemently. Wilma stopped in her tracks.

The smile she had on her face suddenly vanished. David looked pale and tired.

"Whatever is the matter?" "I have a little head cold, that's all. I don't want you to catch it. Anyway, I wanted you to be the first to know, that I have decided to tell your husband about our indiscretion." Wilma laughed. "Really? Is that what you're calling it? What would make you do such a thing after all these years?"

"I'm sorry Wilma, I have to. I have no choice. I have not been able to forgive myself. Nor have I felt forgiven."

"David, please don't do this. Please!" "Wilma, I can't move on. I can't get past it." "David it happened a million years ago. Why now?"

"It's time." "I don't believe you would ruin my life because you can't get past it. I don't believe it! Don't you know you would also ruin your own life in the process? What will happen to the church? What about your wife? What about your son? You don't expect my husband to keep this scandal a secret do you?"

David dropped his head as he told Wilma his decision was final and there was nothing she could do or say to change his mind.

"Okay, okay, do what you have to," she said with her arms raised in defeat. She turned abruptly and walked out of the kitchen, through the back door and out into the night.

Wilma couldn't allow David to destroy her life. She knew she had to stop him, by any means necessary!

Chapter 22

By Any Means Necessary

*W*ilma road around for a while. She had to find a way to keep Pastor Dillion's mouth shut. She was not about to let him ruin the life she had grown accustomed to.

After several hours of riding and thinking, she had formulated a plan. She decided he would have to be eliminated. Wilma drove herself home and immediately went into her office. She turned on her computer and started looking up fast acting poisons. She decided on cyanide, as it would work in a matter of minutes. She planned to mix a few drops in a cup of tea.

She remembered David was a big tea drinker. He had a cold, so it would be fairly easy to go by the church and take him a thermos of tea with honey, laced with a few drops of the cyanide. She'd discovered in her research, cyanide had the taste and smell of bitter almonds. Wilma decided she would tell him the tea was called almond, honey tea and it was her mother's secret recipe for a bad cold. Even if he only took a sip or two, it would be enough.

Wilma searched the internet until she found a site where she could order the poison. She ordered it and requested next day delivery.

Unable to sleep, she tossed and turned all night. She kept fine tuning her plan over and over in her mind. Just before dawn, she finally drifted off into a deep sleep and slept until well past noon. She was awakened by a sudden light that flooded the room. Opening one eye, she was able to see a figure standing at the window pulling back the curtains and opening the blinds, it was her live-in housekeeper, Nancy.

"Mrs. Wakefield are you okay? It is past noon Ma'am. I've brought you a tray of food.

You must be famished by now." "Thank you," Wilma whispered. She laid there a few more minutes and finally she threw back the covers, swung her legs over the side of the bed, put on her slippers and reached for the robe that graced the foot of the bed.

After putting on her robe, she made her way to the master bathroom. Once she returned to the bedroom, she looked a little more radiant. The housekeeper had set a tray of food on a small round table in front of the window.

She removed the silver plate cover. The appetizing presentation made her realize she was indeed hungry. Her favorite red, white and blue salad; along with some miniature chicken pate sandwiches were on the tray. She started with her coffee and after a few long gulps, she sat the cup down and began to eat from her plate.

It suddenly occurred to her after she'd finished eating, it was her bridge club day. She glanced at the clock on the nightstand and got up and walked to her master bathroom to shower and get dressed.

Wilma stood in the mirror, satisfied with the colorful floral dress she'd chosen from her wardrobe. She picked up a bottle of her favorite perfume from the mirrored tray on her dressing table and began squirting it liberally. Then she used her fingers to fluff her hair in the mirror. Wilma's skin was clear and even. She didn't need much in the way of makeup. A little lipstick, a little mascara and blush on her cheeks and she was ready. She still looked much younger than her age and was proud to show off her beauty.

Grabbing her purse and keys, she was about to run out to the garage to start the car when she remembered her cell phone. She started looking in all the places she usually put it. Glancing at her watch, she realized she didn't have time to look for it. She grabbed the house phone from its cradle and dialed her cell number, listening for the ringtone she had become so accustomed to. Just as she walked past the garage door she heard a faint ring.

Wilma quickly went out the door to the garage and there on the front passenger seat of the car lay her cell phone. "There it is!" She opened the car door to retrieve the phone. Then she quickly hit the panel to open the garage door and jumped in the car. She started the engine, put the car in reverse and backed out of the driveway, using her car camera to guide her.

Wilma had a bad habit of checking her messages while driving. She saw that she had three messages. The first message was from a number that was unfamiliar to her. She waited until she got to the next stop light and clicked on the number to read the message.

"In order to score, you'll find the hands wrapped, tied and placed in a drawer. Hands that brought him pleasure, the left one with a sparkling diamond to treasure. Leaving my arms aching. He should have been mine for the taking. Can't you see? It should have been me!"

The car behind Wilma started blowing his horn, startling her. She put her foot on the gas and sped off. She was distraught by the text message. The only parts of Georgette's body that had not been found yet, were her hands.

She knew she would not be able to concentrate on a bridge game or anything else for that matter. Instead, she turned the car around, picked up her phone and began dialing one of the girls to say something had come up and she wasn't going to make it after all.

Afterward, she called her daughter, Diana. "Hello, Di?" "Hello, Mother. What's up?" "I was wondering if I could come over. I received a text message just a little while ago. It was quite disturbing." There was no sound, "Di, did you hear me?" "Yes Mother, I heard you." "Can I come over?" "Of course, Mother, of course you can." "Okay, I'm on my way."

Twenty minutes later, Wilma was pulling into Diana's driveway. She jumped out of her car and ran up the steps to the front door. Before she could ring the bell, the door flew open and Diana was standing there. "Come in Mother." "I'm so sorry dear to come on such short notice, I didn't know where else to turn."

"No worries, I'm glad you came. Is the message another clue about Georgette's case?" "Yes, it is." Wilma reached in her purse and pulled out her phone. She showed Diana the text message she had received.

Diana gasped. "I think we should call Detective Griffin."

A short time later, the bell rang and Diana went to answer the door. It was Detective Griffin. "Hello Ma'am, I came as quickly as I could. What's so urgent?" Diana thanked him for coming and led him into the kitchen. He greeted Wilma Wakefield as he entered the room. "Hello Ma'am, nice seeing you again." "Hello Detective. I'm afraid we have some distressing news for you." She leaned over the table and handed him her cell phone so he could read the text message.

The detective read the message. "I'm not too surprised. After all, I didn't think it was likely we wouldn't receive word regarding the hands as it's the only part of the body unaccounted for. At least now we have a small clue that will hopefully lead us to where the hands are."

Detective Griffin turned to leave, "I'll call you if I find out anything." He walked out the door and closed it behind him.

Chapter 23

David's Demise

*W*ilma showered and dressed early the next morning. She waited anxiously for the mailman to come. She knew he would have to ring the doorbell to get her signature.

She'd forgotten that part. How could she be so stupid not to realize the package containing the cyanide poisoning could lead back to her? She was uneasy and jittery. She paced up and down trying to think of a story to cover her tracks should the need arise.

At any rate, there was no indication that David's demise could lead the police to even suspect her. She thought they had been very careful over the years not to draw attention to themselves by doing anything that might connect them to each other. She was reasonably sure that no one saw her visit him the few times she came to the church to talk to him about Georgette.

Fortunately, it was the housekeeper's day off and she had left the premises to visit her family. The mailman came early and Wilma scribbled an illegible signature on his signature pad, took the package and closed the door.

She had already brewed the tea and put it in the thermos. She only needed to add a few drops of the poison to it. With a deep breath, she picked up the package of disinfectant wipes she'd purchased the day before and put them in her purse. Afterward, she took her purse, her keys and the thermos and left the house.

Wilma hoped she would not encounter anyone at the church. She parked her car a block away and walked the short distance, carrying the thermos of tea in a bag. She looked around every so often to see if she saw anyone about. She didn't. She walked right up to the front door of the church and taking one last look around, entered into the sanctuary.

Luckily, there was no one about. Wilma walked straight through to the church offices. Tiptoeing toward Pastor Dillion's office, she put her ear to the door. She could hear the sound of typing on the computer.

She looked down the hall, seeing no one; she knocked very softly on the door and walked in without waiting for a reply. She closed the door quietly behind her. David looked up from the computer with a surprised look on his face. "Wilma what are you doing here?" "Oh I just dropped by to bring you a thermos of my mother's famous bitter almond and honey tea. It doesn't taste that good but it sure works well for knocking a cold out in no time."

"Well thanks, that's very thoughtful of you. However, in the future for both of our sakes; please don't come here unless you have come to use the sanctuary for prayer or you have some important church business to discuss. I don't want people getting the wrong idea."

"Your right, I wasn't thinking. I just wanted to help you feel better, that's all." Wilma unscrewed the top and poured the tea into the thermos cup. "This will fix you right up. She sat the thermos cup in front of him and he picked it up and took one sip. He frowned and said, "This tea taste awful." "Wilma laughed, "I know, but trust me, you will feel like a new man by morning." Pastor David took one more sip and said, "As bad as it tastes, I'd better." He sat the thermos cup down on his desk.

Wilma walked behind him "Why David, you look so tense, let me massage your neck, it will loosen you up a bit." Pastor Dillion didn't reply. Instead his head began to slowly move forward until he fell facedown onto the keyboard.

Wilma placed two fingers on the side of his neck. She felt no pulse. Lifting his right hand from his lap, she took his pulse from the wrist. Still nothing. Pastor David Dillion was dead.

Wilma removed the package of disinfectant wipes from her purse, she opened the package and withdrew several wipes, using them to wipe down everything she'd touched. She picked up the thermos cup, poured the rest of the tea back into the thermos, screwed the top on, and put it back in the bag she brought it in. She then used the wipes to clean the door knob inside and out. Looking out into the hallway and seeing no one, she walked out of the office and used the wipes to close the door behind her. She put the used wipes inside of the bag with the thermos and walked quickly and quietly out through the sanctuary to the front door.

Seeing no one, she walked down the street to her car. She drove to the town junkyard, threw the bag containing the thermos and used wipes onto one of the trash heaps and drove off.

Chapter 24

Bethany's Discovery

*B*ethany woke up to the sound of the alarm clock ringing. She reached over to turn it off and threw back the covers to get up from, what proved to be another night of restless off and on sleep. It was about five in the morning before she was able to succumb completely.

This situation had been going on since she and David met Marcus and his fiancé at the restaurant. He had been careful to keep his distance from her since that day. She knew something was bothering him. She just didn't know what.

She had tried waiting up for him each night but he made sure not to come home from the church until very late. He had been sleeping in the guest bedroom and it seemed whenever she would go down the hall to talk to him about the situation, he would pretend to be asleep. She told herself she would catch him in the morning at breakfast, but each day he hurried out the door without eating.

Bethany rarely went by the church during the week. After all she had her own work and kept herself busy with meetings and outreach ministry. She threw herself into these, and other projects with fervor in order to keep her mind off of what was going on.

However, today she decided enough was enough and she planned to go to the church and get to the bottom of things. She was determined to confront him about his strange behavior.

After she showered and dressed she called the church office, but got no answer. She then called Marcus' office phone to see if he knew where his father was. There was no answer from his phone either.

Bethany concluded they were in another part of the church and resolved she was going to the church and wait for David to come back to his office no matter how long it took.

Once she was on her way, Bethany dialed Marcus's cell phone again. He answered just before she was about to hang up. "Hello Mother." "Hello Dear." I was wondering if you could tell me where your father might be."

Marcus paused, "I'm not sure, I took the day off and I didn't go by the church this morning." "Oh, okay then. If you hear from him, please tell him I'm trying to reach him." "Yes, I will," Marcus said.

Bethany didn't tell Marcus she was already on her way to the church. When she arrived, she pulled into a parking space in the front and got out. For some reason, she had a knot in her throat and her stomach was doing flip flops. Bethany hated confrontation and mostly avoided it whenever possible, but today she felt it was necessary to clear the air and she was glad that Marcus would not be there.

Bethany walked through the sanctuary to the door that led to the church offices. When she was just outside of David's door, she took a deep breath, closed her eyes and said a silent prayer, asking the Lord to be with her and give her the right words to say.

She knocked on the door softly and listened for his voice. Hearing nothing, she turned the knob and pushed the door open. To her surprise, David was slumped over his desk. His eyes were opened and his face was pale. "David, are you alright?" Bethany rushed to his side and shook him lightly. His body fell limply to the right side, lifeless.

Without so much as taking her husband's pulse, she knew he was dead. Bethany began to scream. She ran from the room, down the hall back through the sanctuary and out the front door. She was hysterical. Shaking and crying, she nervously dialed 9-1-1 on her cell phone.

When the police came about ten minutes later, Bethany was sitting in her car looking stone faced. Detective Griffin was parking his car behind the two squad cars. The police ran up the steps to the church and Detective Griffin walked over to Bethany's car and knocked on the window. She turned slowly toward him and pointed to the church. "He's in there," she said. The tears were still fresh on her face.

The detective handed her a handkerchief and she took it and covered her face as she began to sob uncontrollably.

More police cars came and the church was sealed off in yellow tape. They were ordered by the detective to search every inch of the church from top to bottom. Detective Griffin had a hunch. He didn't know why, just a gut feeling they would find something.

After searching Pastor Dillion's office, they searched Marcus' office next. They began by searching each and every desk drawer. Finally, the bottom drawer on the right side of the desk had a package inside. It was wrapped in butcher paper and tied with a string.

Detective Griffin used his pen knife to cut the string and began unwrapping the package. There in the center of the package lay a pair of bloody hands. The detective looked at one of the officer's standing nearby, "Well what do you know?" The other officer gasped.

After many hours of searching the church, one of the officers was tasked with taking Mrs. Dillion home. Detective Griffin went to Marcus' apartment looking for him. When he didn't answer, they had the landlord to provide them entry to the property. They went in and searched everywhere. They found his digital camera and took it as evidence once they viewed the pictures of Georgette on it multiple times. Finally, they concluded their search. They left the premises and locked the door.

Detective Griffin had tried without success to reach Marcus on his cell phone. He finally had to put out an 'All Points Bulletin' for him.

As the detective was leaving, he dialed Diana Wakefield on his cell phone to let her know he believed the missing pair of hands were found. He asked her to wait until morning before coming down to the coroner's office again to see if she could identify the hands as Georgette's.

He didn't share much with her regarding the details, but the case was progressing far beyond what Diana knew. It could wait until morning. Instead, he went home to a hot shower, a pastrami sandwich and a cold beer before falling asleep in front of the television.

Chapter 25

An Unexpected Turn of Events

*J*onathan arrived at the bank early. He wanted to get a jump start on the day. His only stop was at his favorite coffee house, several blocks from the bank. Whenever he didn't have breakfast at home before going to work, he would often treat himself to a strong Caramel Macchiato with whipped cream and a blueberry muffin.

When he arrived at the bank, he parked his car in the space with his name on it and got out of the vehicle. He carried his bag filled with the morning's nourishment and his keys in one hand while holding his briefcase in the other.

He hadn't been himself lately and made a mental note to ask his secretary to schedule an appointment with his doctor. Today was no different. He was experiencing mild chest pains but had not said anything to Wilma about it. He didn't want her fussing over him or nagging him about what he ate.

He sat his briefcase and breakfast bag on the bench and used his bank keys to unlock the door. After unlocking the door, he put the keys in his pocket and picked up the briefcase along with his breakfast.

Once inside, he disarmed the bank's security alarm system and began turning on the lights. The security guard was not scheduled to arrive for another 45 minutes. Jonathan enjoyed the time he had alone before the staff and security came. He put his breakfast bag on the desk, sat down and put his briefcase underneath the desk.

He began taking his coffee and muffin out of the bag and enjoyed that first sip from his cup to the fullest. He finished his muffin and coffee and wiped his mouth and hands with the napkin. He was about to put the empty cup back in the bag and throw it in the trash when he experienced a very sharp chest pain that rendered him helpless. He was literally unable to move. His eyes rolled to the back of his head as another sharp pain gripped his body. Jonathan grabbed his chest. He reached for the phone on his desk but just as he picked up the receiver, another sharp pain pierced through his body. He slumped over the desk still holding the telephone receiver.

Ironically, Jonathan died just as his Father before him. A heart attack took them both while sitting at the same desk at the same bank.

The security guard came in 30 minutes later. Walking past the glass enclosed office, he saw the bank president slumped over his desk. Immediately he ran into the office, took his pulse, and after what seemed like a very long minute he concluded there was none. Taking the telephone receiver from Jonathan's hand, he dialed the Coroner's office.

Chapter 26

History Repeats Itself

*W*hen the attorney read Jonathan's Will, like Jonathan's father before him, he'd left the bank and the bulk of his empire to his daughter, Diana. Just as his father had left the bank to him.

The attorney directed his next words towards Wilma as he read the section of the Will that pertained to her. He left her the house they lived in. Jonathan had written in the Will a reminder to Wilma of the terrible argument they had that night when he discovered he was not Georgette's biological father. He'd never told her he knew. He also reminded her of his final words that evening as he ascended up the staircase to the bedroom, when he paused and turned to her saying "No worries, it will all balance out in the end."

After he read those words from Jonathan's Will, the attorney removed the last two sealed closed documents left in the folder. One was addressed to the attorney, he took that one and put it in his inside jacket pocket to open later. The other envelop was for Wilma. He handed it to her. She opened it and inside was the deed to the house and a key to his safe deposit box. At that point, the attorney concluded the reading of the Will.

Everyone left the attorney's office. Wilma thought surely there would be stocks, bonds, other property deeds and assets stored in the safe deposit box for her. She didn't much care about the bank going to her daughter Diana. She deserved it, she was a good girl and had never given them an ounce of trouble.

Wilma went directly to the bank after she left the attorney's office. She was anxious to see what other assets Jonathan had left for her.

Once she was in the small private room of the bank vault, the bank officer handed her the matching key and left the room. Wilma was shaking as she opened the box. Inside was one document. She opened the document and read it. It was the DNA results that confirmed Jonathan was not Georgette's father. It was dated many years earlier, when Georgette was just a baby.

Wilma gasped! He knew all this time and never said a word! She turned the box upside down, shaking it as if she expected more.

What irony! Even from the grave, Jonathan was able to get his long awaited revenge for what Wilma had done to him.

Wilma stood there stunned. At that moment, all she could think about was David, the man of God and how she took his life to protect her own, all for nothing! She thought to herself, *what have I done? What have I done?*

The tears ran down her cheeks and for the first time, she had no words. No words at all.

Chapter 27

The Conclusion of the Matter

*T*he attorney waited for everyone to leave before he pulled the envelope from his pocket. Stapled to the front was a note with instructions that stated where the attorney was to deliver the envelope and who he was to give it to.

The attorney put the envelope back in his jacket pocket and proceeded to gather his belongings. He placed them inside of his briefcase and left the building.

He wondered what the envelope contained, but as a man of integrity he didn't open it to find out. When he arrived at the appointed destination, he walked through the door and headed straight to the Desk Sergeant.

The Sergeant looked up and asked, "Can I help you?" The attorney introduced himself as he reached in his jacket pocket to hand the Desk Sergeant his business card. He stated he had an envelope for Detective Griffin. "He's busy at the moment. I'll be happy to give it to him." The attorney shook his head and stated his instructions were to see Detective Griffin and give the envelope to him only.

"Suit yourself," the Sergeant said, with a smirk on his face. "You can have a seat over there. I'll let you know when he is free." The attorney thanked him as he walked toward the bench and sat down.

About 20 minutes later, the Desk Sergeant let the attorney know Detective Griffin was free and he would escort him to the back. Detective Griffin stood up from his desk when the attorney arrived. He introduced himself and the detective asked him to have a seat. "So what brings you here today?"

"I have an envelope from a deceased client who has instructed me to hand deliver it to you, and you alone upon his death." The attorney handed the detective the envelope.

The detective took the envelope, reached for a letter opener and slit it open. He unfolded the fat contents. It was very neatly handwritten and at the very top, in big bold letters it read: Statement of Confession. The detective read the 4 page document in its entirety. It began with the words, "I Jonathan Wakefield, being of sound mind and body, do hereby confess to the murder of Georgette Wakefield."

The detective, was shocked! His investigation into Georgette's murder had led him in a totally different direction. He was almost positive Marcus Dillion was the perpetrator.

His mouth dropped open as he read the entire document and then read it over again.

Jonathan Wakefield stated that Georgette had come to his office to see him one night when he was working late and everyone else had gone home for the day. It was the evening after Valentine's Day. He wrote:

"She was visibly distraught and confessed to me that she was in love with the Pastor's son, Marcus Dillion and they were engaged to be married. She told me how they had met with Marcus' parents over lunch the previous day, seeking their blessing. Instead, their plan to marry was met with disdain. Not from Mrs. Dillion, but from her husband, Pastor David Dillion. He was dead set against it and made no bones about it."

The confession went on to say, "Georgette was crushed. She knew I was a powerful and influential man and she thought perhaps I would be able to convince Pastor Dillion that they were right for each other. Of course Georgette was not aware that I was not her real father, nor did she know that I always suspected Pastor Dillion could very well be her biological father.

I advised Georgette not to pursue the relationship, that I was in agreement Marcus was most likely not the man for her.

Georgette was shocked at my response. She wanted to know what made me say such a thing. She thought surely I would be on her side. Instead, she felt I was leaning on the side of Pastor Dillion and I just didn't want her and Marcus to be together.

She became very angry and began screaming and cursing at me. She picked up the paper weight from my desk and threw it at me, barely missing me by a fraction of an inch.

I grabbed her by the shoulders and began forcefully shaking her, telling her to stop acting like a child. She started beating her fist against my chest and I pushed her away very hard to escape her barrage of punches.

Georgette fell backward, hitting her head on the corner of the desk. Her body convulsed momentarily and then she was still.

I hadn't meant to hurt her. I just wanted to strongly discourage her from marrying a man that might possibly be her own brother."

The statement went on to say that Jonathan didn't know what to do, he was about to call the police when the phone on his desk rang. When he picked up the phone, it was none other than Marcus Dillion.

Marcus wanted to know why his loan had been denied. He knew his proposal and bank records were thorough and in order, he knew he should have qualified. What he didn't know is why Jonathan denied the loan.

Jonathan broke down, he began crying and telling Marcus everything about him not being Georgette's father and how he had suspected Pastor Dillion of being Georgette's father. He confessed to Marcus that Georgette had come to see him and she was now lying in a heap on the floor in front of his desk. He confessed he had DNA results that proved he was not Georgette's father and he felt strongly that Marcus's father was in fact Georgette's father.

Marcus, told Jonathan he was on his way and not to do anything until he arrived. He hung up and ran out of his office to the storage closet. There he retrieved some heavy duty garbage bags and some duct tape.

Marcus hurried out of the backdoor of the church to his car and drove hurriedly to the bank. He was distraught over Georgette's death. He now believed Georgette was the child born out of wedlock to his father and Wilma Wakefield that Cynthia talked about. No wonder his father was so adamant that he not marry Georgette, he knew she was his sister.

At the same time, he was formulating a plan in his mind. The plan could possibly help his mother to escape the disgrace his father had caused by committing adultery.

He decided he would help Jonathan to get rid of Georgette's body in exchange for his reversal of the loan denial decision. This way, he could silence Cynthia and keep her from spreading information to the media about his father's sexual encounter with Mrs. Wakefield. He knew his Mother would be devastated if she knew. He wanted to spare her the embarrassment, if at all possible. She had put her heart and soul into ministering to the women of this community and he didn't want anything to tarnish the reputation and comradery she'd worked so hard to build.

Chapter 28

Partners in Crime

*M*arcus arrived at the bank and parked his car around the back entrance. He got out with the bags and the duct tape and walked up to the door. He knocked on the door and Jonathan came to the door with bloodshot eyes, looking haggard. He unlocked the door and let Marcus in.

Marcus didn't mince words. He instantly told Jonathan of his plan to dispose of Georgette's body in exchange for the bank loan. Jonathan agreed. He made out a bank check for fifty thousand dollars and handed it to Marcus.

Marcus was distracted at that moment by the site of Georgette lying on the floor. He found himself overwhelmed with grief seeing her like that. He sat down on the floor beside her.

Putting his arms around her, he held her close as the tears ran down his face. He began rocking her back and forth as he whispered, "I'm so sorry. This would have never happened had it not been for me. Jonathan cleared his throat and Marcus looked up to see him standing there holding the check with tears in his eyes. Marcus took the check and slid it into his pocket.

When they had finally gotten themselves together, they both began to cut the side seams of the heavy duty garbage bags, laying them out and duct taping them together until they had a large canvas of the heavy duty plastic. They gently laid Georgette's body at the edge of the plastic cover and began to roll her up inside. They folded and taped the ends closed and wrapped tape around the middle section of the bundle.

Marcus pointed his car key Fob toward the back door. After hearing the lock disengage, he used the Fob again to pop the hood of the trunk. Both men bent down simultaneously and lifted Georgette's body at either end. They carried her remains through the back door and loaded her into the trunk of Marcus' car.

Marcus turned to Jonathan and told him to wipe down all the surfaces of his office and clean the blood stain from the corner of his desk where Georgette hit her head. Then lock up and go home. Jonathan nodded, he turned and walked back inside and Marcus got in the front seat and drove off.

He had no idea how he was going to dispose of the body. For now, he decided to leave it in the trunk for the night hoping he could come up with a plan by morning.

Needless to say, he slept very little. However, by morning he had decided he would talk to Cynthia. He felt if he were going to give her fifty thousand dollars, she should be a part of the solution in helping Marcus to dispose of the body. He decided he would show her the check he had gotten from Jonathan and tell her he would give her the fifty thousand dollars and also keep the extra five thousand he had already given her if she could come up with a plan to dispose of Georgette's body.

Just as Marcus thought, Cynthia was eager to get the money and agreed to come up with a master plan to dispose of Georgette's body.

She remembered the recent breaking news story about a similar M.O. of a serial killer sighted not far from their town and presented the plan to Marcus. Cynthia thought it would be a good idea that would throw the authorities off, sending them on a wild goose chase. She also told him about her idea to solicit the butcher she bought meat from in her neighborhood to help them to cut the body up and attach messages to each part.

Marcus was against the idea at first but Cynthia was able to convince him that it was the only way they could steer attention away from all those who were involved. Finally, she wore him down and he agreed.

Cynthia volunteered to write the messages, not realizing that in doing so, her emotions would get the better of her. In the end, she would be caught up and consumed with revenge so deep, her only focus was to incriminate the man she wanted but could not have. Even though Georgette was gone, Marcus could think of nothing else. He continued to thwart every advance Cynthia made.

Cynthia knew the butcher would be more than willing to participate in her plan to dismember the body and distribute the parts, a little at a time to different locations throughout the town.

He made it known to her many times that he liked her. He was not Cynthia's type though. He was a chubby guy with thinning hair. His apron was always filthy. In fact he had never been able to get a girlfriend and would have done anything for Cynthia just to have a chance to be with her.

He would always give her extra meat whenever she came to his shop for steaks, and chicken. She planned to make him an offer he couldn't refuse in exchange for his help.

She was sure her idea would draw attention away from any possible suspects the police could conjure up among them. It would also direct their attention to the possibility of the work being that of the serial killer who used the same M.O. they planned to implement.

Chapter 29

Guilty by Association

*T*he police found and arrested Marcus. After 48 hours of grueling interrogation, he agreed to turn State's evidence. He would have to write a statement describing the part each person involved played in the murder and dismemberment, the writing and planting of the messages as well as placement of the body parts of Georgette. In return, Marcus would receive a one year probation. The other accomplices would be charged accordingly and would serve time for their participation.

Marcus agreed and was given a pen and paper to write a full statement. Marcus wrote how after business hours, Cynthia's butcher cut up Georgette's body with an old electric meat cutting machine and some sharp knives he had stored in the basement of the meat market.

He was a willing participant and had been promised a night of pleasure with Cynthia after the job was completed.

They left Marcus in the interrogation room for several hours after he had completed his statement. When they finally came to unlock the door and lead him to a cell, he saw Cynthia and the butcher standing in the detective's office with their hands handcuffed behind their backs.

Detective Griffin called Diana Wakefield and told her the case had been solved and he would come by to tell her the details. But Diana couldn't wait. She decided to go down to the precinct and see the detective that day.

It just so happened, when she arrived she saw Cynthia, Marcus and another man she did not know. She was puzzled to see her best friend standing there with her hands cuffed behind her back.

She walked up to Cynthia and asked her what was going on. Cynthia looked at Diana and said, "I'm sorry Di." She shrugged her shoulders before speaking again, "Nothing personal against your sister, it was just business."

Diana looked at Cynthia with distaste. "You witch!" She reached up and slapped her hard across the face, turned on her heels and stormed out of the building.

Chapter 30

It is Well

*W*ilma Wakefield was found sitting up in bed with her hair and makeup flawlessly executed. She wore a beautiful white nightgown and her most expensive cultured pearls embellished her neck.

On the nightstand beside her bed sat a cup of tea. The stain of her lipstick was left on the rim of the teacup. The smell of bitter almonds was still present in the air.

A suicide note was propped up against the lamp on the nightstand. It was written on her prettiest stationary and addressed to her daughter Diana. It simply said, "Dear Diana, I'm so sorry, dear. I realize that most of the pain you had to endure was due to the mistakes I made. You didn't deserve the heartache you went through. Out of everyone, I believe you suffered the most and deserved it the least. I hope you can forgive me. I love you so much. I can't bear to watch the pain and suffering that is apparent in your countenance due to the loss of your sister, your father and your best friend. I pray somehow you will find happiness and most of all, you will find peace. Love, Mother."

It was a month since Georgette's case had come to a close. When Diana woke up that Sunday morning, she experienced such a spiritual awakening. She suddenly realized so many deaths had taken place that year, both physical and relational. These deaths were comprised of those she truly loved.

It was indeed a wake-up call. She didn't want it all to be in vain. Somehow she knew something good had to come out of all the chaos that had transpired.

She could hear the church bells ringing from her bedroom. For the first time, she had the strongest urge to get up, shower, dress and go to church, and so she did.

When she arrived, service had just begun. She opened the doors to the sanctuary. Standing there, it seemed as if all eyes were on her.

Diana took a deep breath and walked down the center aisle toward the front. Other than the sound of her high heels clicking against the tile floor as she walked, you could hear a pin drop. She made her way toward the front, found a seat and sat down. The organ music started again and everyone stood to sing:

When peace like a river, attendeth my way, when sorrows like sea billows roll; whatever my lot, thou hast taught me to say,
"It is well, it is well with my soul."
It is well, with my soul.
It is well, it is well with my soul.

After they sang the hymn and sat down, Diana was aware of someone seated next to her. She turned her head to see who it was. It was none other than Detective Griffin. "Why Detective, what a pleasant surprise." "Lance, call me Lance." "Okay Lance." He reached over and slid his hand around hers as the new pastor stood to deliver his sermon. "Open your Bibles please to John 16:33 (NIV). "I have told you these things, so that in me you may have peace. In this world you will have trouble. But take heart! I have overcome the world."

In spite of all she had been through, for the first time in a very long time, Diana felt at peace. She wondered to herself, *what took me so long to come?*

//The End//

Biography

Phyllis Clemmons holds a Bachelor's degree in Business Administration from Faulkner Christian University and a Master's degree from Webster University in Management, Human Resource Development and Leadership.

She is an accomplished, self-published author and has been a nominee for the prestigious literary Henri Award three years in a row. In 2016 she won the Reader's Choice Award for her book in the Testimonial genre titled Spirit to spirit.

She has worked in the government, city, private sectors for many years.

Other Books by Phyllis Clemmons

1. Kelsey from Pain to Triumph, 2nd Edition

2. Spirit to spirit

3. Asiah's Everyday Life Picture Poetry Book

4. Draw Near, My Beloved

Made in the USA
Middletown, DE
17 July 2023

35311227R00126